Daniel C. Eddy

Eddy's Travels in Europe

Daniel C. Eddy

Eddy's Travels in Europe

ISBN/EAN: 9783337211899

Printed in Europe, USA, Canada, Australia, Japan

Cover: Foto ©Andreas Hilbeck / pixelio.de

More available books at **www.hansebooks.com**

BY

REV. D. C. EDDY,

AUTHOR OF

"WALTER'S TOUR IN THE EAST"
"TRAVELS IN ASIA AND AFRICA"

BOSTON.
CHARLES E. BROWN & CO.

TABLE OF CONTENTS.

	PAGE
THE TRIANGLE FORMED	9

A Talk with Rip Van Winkle. — Will, Fred and Charlie. — Arrangements with the Travelling Correspondent. — Sailing of the Master.

RIP VAN WINKLE IN IRELAND 14

Queenstown. — Cork. — Shandon, Dublin, Drogheda. — Dean Swift. — Trinity College. — Belfast.

RIP VAN WINKLE IN SCOTLAND 32

The Clyde. — Glasgow. — Edinburgh. — Holyrood. — Sir Walter Scott. — Melrose. — John Knox. — Burns.

RIP VAN WINKLE IN ENGLAND 43

London. — Oxford. — Exeter. — Leeds. — Birmingham. — Newcastle. — York. Sheffield. — Bedford. — Liverpool.

RIP VAN WINKLE IN FRANCE 76

Paris. — Palaces. — The Triumphal Arch. — Fontainebleau. — Versailles. — Lyons. Avignon. — Rouen. — Amiens. — Marseilles.

RIP VAN WINKLE IN ITALY 108

Genoa. — Naples. — Pompeii. — Vesuvius. — Rome. — St. Peter's. — The Vatican. The Forum. — Florence. — Venice. — Verona. — Milan. — Pisa.

RIP VAN WINKLE IN SWITZERLAND 180

The Simplon. — Brieg. — Swiss Colleges. — The Glaciers. — Geneva. — Lausanne. The Rigi. — Berne.

CONTENTS.

	PAGE
RIP VAN WINKLE IN GERMANY	195

Berlin. — Dresden.— Green Vaults. — Hamburg. — Heidelberg. — Wittenberg. Adelsberg.— Vienna.— Frankfort.— Luther.

RIP VAN WINKLE IN BELGIUM AND HOLLAND 220

Brussels. — Hotels. — Waterloo. — Amsterdam. — Canals. — Rotterdam. — The Hague. — Haarlem. — Leyden. — Dort.

RIP VAN WINKLE IN DENMARK, NORWAY AND SWEDEN . . 235

Higher Latitudes. — Copenhagen. — Christiania. — Stockholm. — The Dunes. Public Education. — Manners and Customs.

RIP VAN WINKLE IN RUSSIA 250

Alexander II. — St. Petersburg. — The Tragedy. — Moscow — The Kremlin. Cronstadt. — Warsaw. — St. Ivan.

RIP VAN WINKLE IN TURKEY 262

The Golden Horn.—Constantinople.—The Mosques.—The Streets,—St. Sophia. The Seraglio. — The Bosphorus. — The Black Sea.

RIP VAN WINKLE IN GREECE 270

Piræus. — The Acropolis. — Mars Hill.— The Parthenon. —The Stadium. —The Temple of Herod. — Athens as it is.

RIP VAN WINKLE IN SICILY 283

Messina — Palermo. — Reggio.— Syracuse. — Etna. — Stromboli. — Products of Sicily.— Meeting with Scapegrace.

RIP VAN WINKLE IN PORTUGAL 292

Gibraltar. — Lisbon. — The City Streets. — The Palaces. — Condition of the People. — Social Customs. — Productions.

RIP VAN WINKLE IN SPAIN 296

Cadiz.—Malaga.— Granada.—Seville.—Cordova.

LIST OF ILLUSTRATIONS.

	PAGE		PAGE
The Alcazar, Seville	1	Lyons	95
On the Lee	9	Avignon	96
Shandon	14	St. Ouen, Rouen	97
Queenstown	19	Amiens Cathedral	100
Strand Street, Liverpool	20	Amphitheatre, Nimes	101
The Four Courts	23	Amphitheatre, Arles	102
Dean Swift's Birthplace	25	Mont St. Michel	103
Grafton Street, Dublin	26	Notre Dame de la Garde	104
The Clyde near Coulter	32	Peasant at Home	106
Glasgow	33	A Fernch School	107
Douglas Castle	36	The Capitol	108
Oaks at Bradgate	43	Genoa from the Heights	109
Exeter	46	Vesuvius	112
The Guildhall, Exeter	47	The House of the Questor	118
Exeter Cathedral	50	Baker's Oven and Bread	119
Town Hall, Birmingham	59	General View of Pompeii	121
Birmingham	60	House of Panza	123
Coventry	62	Clearing a Street	126
Exeter Cathedral—West Front	63	Searching for Remains	129
Gateway, Jesus College	64	Street in Pompeii	132
King's College	65	Gate of Herculaneum	135
Elstow Church	66	Arch of Septimius Severus	141
Statue of Bunyan	67	Castle of St. Angelo	147
Palace of the Trocadero	76	In the Forum	148
Paris Bread-Carrier	79	The Mamertine Prison	149
Old Paris	81	St. Peter's and the Vatican	153
Cathedral of Notre Dame	83	Papal Benediction	155
Cathedral of St. Denis	85	On the Campagna	157
Hotel des Invalides	87	Castle of San Elmo	163
Old Houses	88	Getting ready for a Start	169
Depot of Tract Society	89	Florence	171
Tower of St. Jacques	91	The Baptistery, Pisa	172
Fontainebleau	93	The Gondola	175

LIST OF ILLUSTRATIONS.

	PAGE		PAGE
Cathedral of St. Mark	177	Cathedral at Copenhagen	241
On the Grand Canal	178	The Vettifas	242
Torchlight on the Swiss Lakes	180	The Bourse	243
Châlets near Sepey	181	Norwegian Wedding	244
Brieg on the Simplon	184	Castle of Rosemborg	245
Railway up the Rigi	185	Camp in the Forest	246
Lausanne	186	Transportation	247
On the Mer de Glace	188	Swedish Lovers	248
Vitznau Station on the Rigi	189	Sleighing	250
Valley of Chamouni	190	Siberian Travelling	253
Trying a Glissade	191	Siberian Wedding	255
Basle	193	Ice Transportation	257
High Street, Berne	194	Street Scene	259
Statue of Frederick the Great	197	Turkish Mosque	262
Statue of Frederick Augustus	199	Temple of Sunium	270
Bridge over the Elbe	201	The Piræus	273
Statue of Charles V.	203	The Acropolis	275
Canal at Hamburg	205	The Parthenon	277
Hamburg Market Woman	207	Greek Water-Carriers	278
Heidelberg	208	The Temple of Herod	279
Bacharach	209	Pozzuoli	281
Heidelberg Bridge	210	Stromboli	283
Rat-Catcher's House	211	Sicilian Costumes	285
Wittenberg Market-Place	213	Chapel of Santa Rosalia	287
The Dragon Fountain	214	Syracuse	289
Cavern of Adelsberg	215	Great Mosque, Cordova	290
Luther's House	218	Barcellos	292
Jews' Quarter	219	Gibraltar	293
Windmills for Drawing off Water	220	Fish Merchants	295
Rotterdam ; The Old Harbor	226	Tower of Belem	297
Interior of a Dutch House	227	Rue Neuve des Anglais, Oporto	299
Amsterdam	229	The Giralda	301
Lime Market	231	The Court of Oranges	302
The Poor District	233	The Spanish Postilion	303
Bergen	235	The Muleteer of Granada	304
Notre Dame	237	Honey-seller of Madrid	306
Interior of Notre Dame	239	Royal Palace	307
Street in Christiania	240	The Bull-fight	308
Winter Palace	240	Leaning Tower, Saragossa	312

RIP VAN WINKLE AWAKE.

ON THE LEE.

RUPERT VAN WERT was the master of a school in one of the suburbs of New York. He had, on leaving college, founded this institution of learning, and somewhat ambitiously named it "THE POLYTECHNIC," and under his rule it had grown to be worthy of the designation. The master was universally beloved by his pupils, who were gathered from city and country. We should be obliged to go far back to find the origin of the nickname which his boys had good-naturedly substituted for the aristocratic "Van Wert." But however it came, it clung to him, though few teachers in the land could be found to whom it was so little applicable, if Rip Van Winkle represents a sleepy character.

Master Van Wert had dismissed his school for the last time. Twenty-five years he had come and gone with each school-term, without one day of sickness or one serious trouble in his "little kingdom," as he called his school. By frugal living he had amassed a little fortune in his laborious pursuit; and now, weary with the toil, had surrendered the institution to other hands, that he might spend a few years in foreign lands. It cost him many a pang to surrender to younger men the school which he had founded and nursed; but the silver in his hair, though he was not old, admonished him of the flight of time, and reminded him that now, if ever, he must carry out his life-long plan of a journey around the world.

With slow and silent steps he had turned from the throne of his power, and shut the gates of his little kingdom after him, and was sadly walking down the shady avenue, with his hands behind him, when his attention was arrested by the cheerful voice of one of his pupils.

"Master Van Wert!"

It was Charlie, one of his most beloved scholars, that hailed him.

"Master Van Wert!"

The sadness passed away from the master's face, and a pleasant smile overspread his handsome countenance, as he turned and faced his little friend.

"What now, my boy?"

"Why, sir, we all know that you are going abroad, to visit the countries of the old world, and see the places famous in history; and we have formed a society which we propose to call 'The Triangle.'"

"The what?"

"The Triangle, sir."

"Well, who are *we?* and what is 'The Triangle' to be? and what does it propose to do?"

"Oh, sir, *we* are Will, Hal, and I. 'The Triangle' is a society of three."

"Oh, I see, a mathematical society."

"No, sir, a literary society, to meet monthly, and read such letters as you may be pleased to send us."

"So you suppose your old master will write to you every month for the two or three years that he may be absent."

"Such is the humble petition of 'The Triangle,' which I am deputed and authorized to present to you."

"Well, my lad, you might have organized a society for a much worse purpose than that; and as I shall travel very leisurely from place to place, and as writing down my impressions will serve to deepen them in my own mind, and stamp the pictures of foreign life upon my own memory, I will agree to do as you request. On landing in Europe, I will commence my work, and send you a monthly budget, and continue to do so as long as I am on that continent; and if my jottings and pencillings, pen sketches and pictures, prove of sufficient interest to you to have them continued while I am on other continents, you may expect to hear from me."

"Good! good! I will give you the thanks of the society in advance."

"To whom shall I send my budget?"

"To me, sir, care of my father."

"Well, you may expect to hear from me in a few weeks—as soon after I reach the shores of the Old World as I have an opportunity to write, and anything to write about. I shall not give you a continuous narrative of my journeys, but pen and picture sketches of such places as I suppose will most interest you."

"But, master, we have voted to call our society after you—the 'Van Wert Triangle.'"

"What do the boys call me behind my back?" asked the master with a smile.

Charlie hesitated.

"I think you know how they put my initials into shape, don't you?"

"Without any wish to injure your feelings or be disrespectful, they call you 'Rip Van Winkle;' but they all admit that you are wide awake. And then they call you that because it is the *nom de plume* under which you are here known as a writer."

"Why don't you call it 'The Rip Van Winkle Triangle?'"

"Oh, that would not be respectful."

"I don't know that I have any serious objection to the use of my name, but suggest that 'The Triangle' would be more simple."

"I will report to the society. But, master, we have done something else — taken another liberty with you."

A happy look came over the master's face as he saw the enthusiasm of the lad. He had confidence in Will, Hal, and Charlie, and during the conversation memory had been taking him back to his earlier years, and bringing up the long-past and almost forgotten scenes when he was a boy; and his heart was stirred as the shadow and sunshine seemed to mingle in his own lost years.

"What other liberty have you taken with me? Is it not enough that you have surreptitiously taken my name and attached it to your society, but must also commit some other atrocity?" asked the genial, good-natured pedagogue, with a mock expression of anger, and holding up his hand as if to repudiate some wrong.

"Oh, all we have done is to vote you into our Triangle as honorary travelling correspondent. That is all."

"And that is enough; but I will accept. Only, tell me first what salary I am to expect for my services abroad. Travelling correspondents are well paid: what am I to have?"

"Well — as — to that, I suppose the salary will be paid in criticisms. You see, I am president, Hal is reader, and Will is to be critic."

"And I am to be the victim! Ah, ha! ha!"

"No, not that. Will will not be very hard on you. Only you must conform to the rules of writing and composition that you have laid down for us."

"I suppose I must try to stand it, only, tell Will to be merciful, for sometimes my letters will be written under great disadvantages and with very poor materials. I will sign my communications, 'RIP VAN WINKLE.'"

"That will be all right, master, only write as often as you can."

The teacher gave a kindly reply and turned away, while Charlie ran off whistling, to meet his companions and tell them of his success with Master Van Wert, or "Rip Van Winkle," as the boys used to call him, and as he signed himself to newspaper and review articles.

And as the boys call him "Rip Van Winkle," so will we; and as we follow him from place to place, we are to find out whether he was asleep or awake. The reader will find this volume to contain a fragmentary account of Rip Van Winkle's travels in Europe, written to "The Triangle" at home. The boys, as we shall see, received the letters, and read them with great interest and attention, discussed the various subjects and places brought to their notice, and criticised them according to the original intentions of the founders of the little reading society composed of the three fast, firm, and true friends, Will, Hal, and Charlie.

IN IRELAND.

SHANDON ON THE LEE.

RIP VAN WINKLE had been gone six weeks when Charlie received a huge letter, upon which he summoned "The Triangle." When the members were all together, the envelope, bearing the English postmarks, was opened, and Hal began to read. He had a fine voice, which, under the Master, had been admirably trained. His reading was always effective, and remarkably so on this occasion, as the well-known handwriting of his friend abroad came under his eye.

BELFAST.

From this fine Irish city I send congratulations to the — the — Triumvirate — no! the Triangle, I think the society was to be called.

You know I sailed from New York in one of the Royal British Steamships, one fine morning a few weeks ago. You were standing on the pier when the noble vessel swung from her moorings and swept down the bay. I saw you waving your handkerchiefs, long after I had ceased to distinguish your faces.

The feeling, on leaving one's own country and friends, is a very sad one, however great may be the pleasure we anticipate, when we lose the features of the kind friends on shore, when we fail to distinguish the forms that stand there waving us, with hat and handkerchief, a last "good-by," and when we turn from the spires of the city, the tall chimneys, and the shining roofs, and look forward to the changes which may occur as the months roll on; "Shall we ever return? shall we ever more meet those kind friends? shall we again behold the spires of yonder city? or, shall we be swallowed up in the deep? or, find a grave in the midst of strangers?" are the questions that, whether we will or not, force themselves upon us, as we leave all behind.

And then to turn from home and friends, from the gay city, and the solid land, and look off upon the ocean, on which no sail is seen, no sign of land in view, nothing but one wide, dreary, billowy waste! It makes one feel as if he were cut off from the rest of the race; as if he stood alone in the wide, wide world; and the feeling of loneliness which creeps over the mind, as he flings himself upon his narrow berth, are sad and oppressive.

But on board the ocean steamers there is a sense of security which relieves the mind of all ideas of present danger. The voyage seems to be in a floating city, lodging at a first-class hotel, and surrounded by first-class companions.

Our ship, though not one of the best or fastest, of the Cunard line of steamers, is a very safe and reliable vessel; and one is amazed to see the operations on board. To go down into the regions occupied by the engine seems like descending into Hades: the blazing fire, the intense heat, the coal-black firemen, who seldom come up into sunlight, the ponderous machinery, and the continual rumbling, hissing, steaming, give an idea of the world of the lost as depicted by poets and orators, and make you feel as if you had reached the infernal regions, and were among the inhabitants of darkness. Dante's Inferno seems to be reached here. About sixty tons of coal per day are consumed, or seven hundred and twenty tons in a voyage of a dozen days. The running expense of the steamer is about five dollars per mile, or nearly fifteen thousand dollars for the whole passage. One hundred and ten men, including officers, cooks, porters, and sailors, are required to convey the huge floating hotel across the deep.

I was surprised at the cooking-department; and with me it was a theme of wonder how, in a little cook-room, food could be furnished for two hundred or three hundred persons, with so much regularity and precision. Much of the time on board is spent in eating. Breakfast at eight o'clock, lunch at twelve o'clock, dinner at four o'clock, tea at seven o'clock, and a late supper between nine and ten o'clock. And my travelling companions had convenient supplies carefully put away. All these meals are furnished with a punctuality and sumptuousness that would do credit to a first-class hotel, and at the table one can hardly discover that he is not at the table of the Astor House, or the St. Nicholas, unless it be by a sudden lurch of the ship, which reminds him of sea-monsters and shipwrecks.

On our outward passage we had little to break the monotony or disturb the quiet of the voyage. On Sunday we had religious services on board, and a naval chaplain preached; and seldom have I seen a more attentive audience. The service was held in the dining-saloon, and about two hundred persons were present. The ship's surgeon read the English church service, that being required by the laws under which these steamers sail. At the close of the reading the sermon was delivered to a mixed company of Christians and infidels, vile and virtuous.

With an excellent commander, an obliging company of servants, a pleasant circle of fellow-passengers, there were few incidents worth the time it would take to relate them. The chief feature of the voyage to me, however, was a fine view of several huge icebergs. The first was seen about dusk on the Saturday evening after leaving home. It was a huge lump of ice, of chalky whiteness, and lay like a rock on the bosom of the deep. It was estimated by competent persons to be about one hundred feet long, and about sixty feet high. It looked cold and cheerless, and had the weather been thick, would have been a very uncomfortable neighbor. The great danger in crossing the Atlantic in the early part of the season arises from two causes — fire and ice. The former, on the British steamers, is provided against. The discipline of the crew, the drill of the commander and officers, the means for extinguishing flame, and the manner in which the vessels are built, make any serious fire almost out of the question. I think it would have been impossible for such a catastrophe to have occurred on board our steamer as swept away the poor, ill-fated Austria, with her incompetent officers and undisciplined crew. But there are scarcely any provisions to be made against contact with ice, except ceaseless vigilance. Should one of these steamers strike an iceberg, with her speed of ten or twelve miles an hour, she would doubtless be destroyed at once. It is supposed that the ill-fated Pacific, one of the Collins line of boats, was lost in this way. The iron steamer Persia, which started from New York about the same time, ran into an iceberg, which providentially happened to have been softened by the action of the sea and air. So great was her speed, and so firm her iron ribs, that she drove into the floating mass of snow and ice nearly one-third of her length, carrying away her wheel-houses, and damaging her most seriously. There she was wedged in with the ice. A critical examination took place, ere any attempt was made to get her off, and fortunately she was found to be firm, and after some hours she was released from her perilous position.

The poor Pacific probably met with a hard iceberg, and at a fearful speed came in collision with it, and was sunk at once, not a single soul returning to tell the fearful tale. In a foggy day or night the iceberg cannot be seen one hundred feet ahead, and as the speed is scarcely slackened, the danger is fearful when the monsters are near. On Sunday morning we saw a huge iceberg, supposed to be about one hundred and fifty feet high, and seven hundred feet long. It had three pinnacles, and the same chalky appearance of the one seen on the previous evening. At four o'clock in the afternoon the cry went through the ship, "An iceberg!" "An iceberg!" and we all rushed on deck to see one directly in our path. It was indeed a most magnificent spectacle. Its proximity to us caused the glass to fall many degrees, and the whole sky assumed a dismal appearance. The sight of this one inhabitant of ocean was worth all the toils and perils of the ocean-voyage. At first it looked like a huge cliff of chalk. As it came nearer its position changed, and it looked like a headless dromedary; then it assumed the appearance of a cluster of round towers set thickly together; and as we sailed within half a mile of it, and had a full, fair view, it took the shape of a dismantled castle. We could seem to see the huge Gothic windows, the high pinnacles, the wide doors, and the lofty proportions of a once elegant structure. It was an immense mass of ice, many times larger than the New York Post Office.

These icebergs, drifting down from the north, and floating into warmer water, are undermined, and at times roll over, with a mighty crash, making the very ocean boil with fury for miles around. It is estimated that at least two-thirds of the ice is below the surface of the water; and one can easily perceive the danger of collision with such a monster. The first view of this sea-demon I shall never forget. Its outlines are now as vivid in my mind as when I was gazing upon it. We soon, however, left it in the distance—the mighty thing which had been forming for hundreds of years in the cold north, was destined to dissolve and mingle with the waters of all seas.

Our steamer took what is called the Northern passage, that is, we went up around the north of Ireland, a passage more dangerous in the winter, but sixty miles shorter than the other. Ireland lies directly in the way of a vessel going to Liverpool from New York, and we are obliged to go around the north or south of it. I had hoped we should have gone to the south, as I wished to have a view of Queenstown, the port of Cork, so called because the present queen landed there on her first visit to Ireland, after her coronation.

QUEENSTOWN.

Our first view of land was obtained early on the morning of our second Sabbath out, and from that time until we reached Liverpool the coastviews of Ireland, Scotland, or Wales were in sight. We entered the river Mersey — a river of the utmost consequence to British commerce — about noon, and came to anchor about the middle of the afternoon, within view of the docks, churches, and houses of Liverpool. The custom-house officials came on board, and after the examination of baggage, the ship's company separated never to meet again in this world.

LIVERPOOL.

Well, we are now in England, and begin our investigations by looking at the docks — huge basins, built of heavy granite blocks. As you approach, the shipping seems to be in the centre of the town, the masts only being seen above the toppling warehouses. Each

STRAND STREET, LIVERPOOL.

dock has its water-gate, and when a vessel wishes to go out, the tide being up, the gate is opened and the ship turned into the river. The extent and magnificence of these docks, which are all surrounded and enclosed with warehouses and stores for the reception of goods, will be understood when I tell you that the Salt-house Dock occupies an area of nearly five acres, and cost three millions of dollars; the Albert Dock covers an area of nearly eight acres, and cost about four million dollars; the King's Dock has an area of more than seven acres, and cost nearly four million dollars; the Queen's Dock has more than ten acres; the Coburg dock has five acres; the Brunswick Dock has nearly thirteen acres, and the construction cost an immense sum of money. There are others of equal extent and magnificence; and these docks are filled with vessels from every land under the sun.

Though not a beautiful city, nor one perfect for residence, Liverpool is not without its attractions in other respects. It has a most magnificent Sailors' Home, where hundreds of poor mariners are saved from destruction. For architectural taste and beauty, we hardly have a building in our city that will equal this benevolent and hospitable residence for the sons of ocean. St. George's Hall, a noble public hall, recently erected for musical entertainments, has no equal in our country. The floors are marble, set in beautiful many-colored mosaics; the walls and ceiling are highly ornamented; the beautiful pillars and arches create a fine effect, while one of the largest organs in the world pours out its rich liquid music over the people.

There are churches and parks, public and private residences, upon which we have no time to linger. The city has grown up to a mammoth community. In 1700 it had only five thousand inhabitants; now it has six hundred thousand. In the year 1812, only four thousand five hundred and ninety-nine vessels, with a tonnage of four hundred and forty-six thousand seven hundred and eighty-eight, entered this port. In 1867, twenty-nine thousand five hundred and fifty-one vessels, with a tonnage of nearly four millions, entered these docks. The revenues at the Liverpool custom-house in 1876 were about thirty millions of dollars, while the annual imports and exports of that city cannot fall much short of two hundred and fifty millions of dollars.

But it was not my purpose to linger long in Liverpool, so we were soon *en route* for Ireland. The ride through North Wales was interesting. The country is very grand, and some parts of it exceedingly beautiful. The villages through which we passed were filled with thatched-roof cottages and a poor but industrious people. Several proud castles lifted their turrets above us as we rushed on, or on the distant hills seemed to stand as sentinels over the surrounding country. We reached the Menai Straits in the evening, but it was light enough to see the Suspension and Tubular bridges. The former is very much like that at Niagara, and is a very noticeable work. The Britannia Tubular Bridge is a great wonder. It is an iron tube, constructed of sheets or plates of iron. These plates are about half an inch thick, and about three feet square, and are closely riveted together, making a square tube wide enough for two trains of cars to pass each other, and high enough to clear the smoke-pipe of the engine. Strong iron knees and braces add to the strength of the tube, so that when the heavy freight-train passes over it, it is not seen to sag or even vibrate. The whole bridge is very long, but the tube is about three hundred feet. It is about one hundred feet from the water below. It was raised to the piers on which it stands by hydraulic pressure, and now, over a fearful chasm, supports itself by its own weight, while trains of cars, heavily freighted with goods and human life, rush wildly through it. The sheets of iron are three in thickness, and yet so riveted as to appear like one. It is doubtless the most wonderful bridge ever built.

We reached Holyhead at eleven o'clock, and went at once on board a steamer bound to Dublin. The night was pitchy dark, and all the accommodations for sleepers were the settees and floors. But we slept well until about four in the morning, when one of our company, who had the nightmare, gave a most unearthly yell, and we all started up, unable to get to sleep again. So we went up on deck, to look out upon the hills of green Erin, and watch for the towers of the city of Dublin. They soon appeared in view; and at six o'clock we stood on Irish soil, in the capital of Ireland.

DUBLIN.

No city that I ever saw surprised me more than Dublin: none disappointed me so much. Though I knew it was called a beautiful city, I had no idea of being compelled to admit that in many respects we have no city in America that equals it. The main street of Dublin, the famous Sackville street, is claimed, and perhaps justly, as being the most beautiful thoroughfare in the world;

THE FOUR COURTS.

and many of the other prominent streets are very fine, and of them the people are justly proud.

The public buildings will compare with those of any city in the world; and we rode from one to another in the light jaunting-car which is peculiar to Ireland. Let me describe it. It is a two-wheeled vehicle, somewhat like an old-fashioned baker's cart which was found in the streets of New England fifty years ago, but which you boys have never seen, with seats on two sides, the people sitting back to back, while the driver is in front. It would be a novelty in Central Park or on Boston Common; but it is just adapted to the wants of the people here. Constructed in a light and easy style, it is a charming carriage to drive about in. In all the places in Ireland which we visited, we found it used by all classes of people, the high and the low, rich and poor. Gay ladies and noble men alike were dashing gayly about from place to place in it; and seldom have I seen any conveyance which pleased me more than this. It is far more graceful and convenient than the cumbersome cab and the lumbering hack of London.

In such a vehicle we drove to the old Cathedral, founded and preached in by St. Patrick. It is a large building, three hundred feet long, considerably decayed. It is hung with the banners of the Knights of Ireland, and the nave is blazoned with coats-of-arms of living Knights of the Order of St. Patrick. In this cathedral is a tablet to the memory of Dean Swift; also one to the memory of an old and faithful servant of the dean, and one to Hester Johnson, the famous Stella of Dean Swift's letters. Beneath the church is a well, in the waters of which St. Patrick consecrated his first Irish convert. From this spot he went forth into all parts of the Green Isle.

Dean Swift's house, or the house where he was born, is not now standing, but we rode to the spot where it once stood, in Hoey's Court, in one of the most wretched parts of the city.

"The Triangle" ought to study the life of Dean Swift as an illustration of the power of mind and laborious study to lift a poor unfortunate child above the accidents of his birth to honor and distinction.

The Bank of Ireland is a noble building, and in the days when Ireland was an independent power, ere England had set her ruthless heel upon the country's neck, was used as a parliament-house. The old hall of commons is now the magnificent banking-room; and instead of Irish orators and statesmen, brokers and merchants meet there in large numbers. The house of lords remains the same as when the lords left it; their vacant chairs, their long table, and the various fixtures of such a room all remain as in the days of Irish power, and the room is used only once a year, — at the annual meeting of the directors of the bank. Where once the throne stood, now stands the statue of an English king. The building covers an area of two and a half acres, and is one of the finest banking-houses in the world, — convenient and spacious within, imposing and grand without.

Near the bank is Trinity College, a vast structure, forming a magnificent quadrangle, and covering an area of several acres. The college was founded by Queen Elizabeth in 1591, and stands on the site of an ancient monastery. The front, facing the college green, is three hundred and eight feet in length, finely and elaborately finished in the highest style of Corinthian taste.

DEAN SWIFT'S BIRTHPLACE.

Chapel, theatre, provost's house, and library, the latter of which is two hundred and seventy feet long, are all furnished with ample apparatus, filled with works of art and science, and enriched with rare histories and manuscripts. In the main square is an elegant bell-tower, ninety-two feet high, which presents to the eye a grand appearance. Some fifteen or sixteen hundred students are here educated, and the whole establishment would make such colleges as Hanover, and such universities as Brown, appear mean and small by the contrast. The college faces the bank, which across the Green, with its magnificent colonnades, its noble Corinthian porticos, its ornamented statues of Hibernia and Fortitude, — the one attended by Fidelity and Commerce, the other by Justice and Liberty, seems to vie with its sister of Intelligence in adorning

GRAFTON STREET, DUBLIN.

the home of O'Connell, the land of Emmet, and a noble company who have gone the way of all the earth.

And the whole city is covered over with noble buildings, of which I have no time to speak, — the Custom House, with its superb dome, its pillars and statues, its antiquated representations, Neptune with his trident, Hope resting on her anchor, and other statues; its four decorated fronts, and the colossal image of Queen Victoria towering above the whole. The Post-Office, a noble Ionic structure, erected at a cost of two hundred and fifty thousand dollars; the huge low buildings known as the Four Courts; the Corn Exchange; the College of Surgeons, and numerous others, are all worthy of any city on the globe.

We took a bird's-eye view of the city from the top of a column erected to the memory of Nelson on Sackville Street. It is one hundred and twenty feet high, and commands a fine view of Dublin and the environs. From that eminence we saw the city like a map spread out before us, — the streets, public buildings, parks, monuments, castles, and various public works.

Having examined the city buildings, we drove about to see the streets. The house where O'Connell lived was pointed out to us, and several other noted houses we saw. We were particularly anxious to see the lower classes, but failed to find anything like Five Points in New York. The worst parts of Dublin were better than portions of New York or Boston; and I left Dublin convinced that for poverty, our own cities are at least equal with it. We hear great accounts of the wretchedness of Ireland. Has not America times of wretchedness? The Irish in this country are far more degraded than those at home, as a general thing, and we err in supposing that there are such extremes of misery in that land.

From Dublin we took the cars northward for Drogheda. This, boys, is a noted old Irish town, of which you have read much in the history of the Irish wars. I wanted to see this town very much, for it has been a familiar name to me for half a century. When a child, I read Cromwell's Life, and there found the account of the terrible siege of that doomed town, and ever since I have desired to see the place. It is some fifty miles or less from Dublin, and we reached it at nightfall, after riding an hour or two through a most lovely country. We found a neat, comfortable, but small inn, and without waiting for supper, began our explorations. It answered my idea of an old Irish town. In a few of the principal streets, are very grand but dingy, gloomy, black-looking brick buildings, while out in the more remote streets are the cabins of the poorer people. We went into some of them, talked with the people, and saw all we could of the forms of life. As one of these cabins will answer for a description of the whole, I present it. It was a cabin inhabited by an old lady of seventy years, her daughter, about twenty-five, a son, and a boarder. The building was an oblong, thirty by fifteen feet. The roof was thatched, the thatching being laid on about one foot thick. This thatching seldom leaks, and will last from four to six years. The straw is placed upon small poles, which serve for rafters. The house is divided into two apartments, by a curtain about six and a half feet high, thus making two rooms about fifteen feet square. The windows were four in number, each about eighteen inches square, the glass in five-inch squares, and the frame set firm in the stone-work of the building. The floor is the bare ground, damp and cold, but hardened. The fireplace is at one end, built of clay and stones, a mere rude pile to put the wood and fire into. The walls were unplastered, but neatly whitewashed; the ceiling was the under side of the thatched roof. A loom for the manufacture of Irish linen was in the room, and a piece of linen was in progress. We were told that a person, by working hard, might earn eight shillings, or two dollars per week!

This cabin is a fair specimen of houses found all over Ireland, and thousands are much more wretched, being built of mud and rushes, and forlorn in the extreme,—nothing but huts. And thus the people live.

There are a few noticeable objects here. Just on one side of the town is what is called the Magdalen Steeple, the large square tower of a noble church. The church fell down four hundred years ago, and yet this steeple still towers aloft, a most beautiful specimen of architecture. It forms an odd, venerable ruin, to which a hundred stories of ghosts and hobgoblins have attached themselves.

This town has had a dreadful history. Its natural and artificial defences were so formidable that Cromwell found it difficult to subdue it. The old stern, iron nature of the Protector had been thoroughly aroused against the Irish people. And he had reason to be aroused. If history has not been perverted, the Puritans, in those fearful times, were treated with most dreadful cruelty. Sir J. Temple, in his "Irish Rebellion," tells us: —

"The Catholics burnt the houses of the Protestants, turned them out naked in the midst of winter, and drove them like herds of swine before them. If, ashamed of their nudity, and desirous of seeking shelter from the rigor of a remarkably severe season, these unhappy wretches took refuge in a barn, and concealed themselves under the straw, the rebels instantly set fire to it, and burned them alive. At other times, they were bound, without clothing, to be drowned in rivers; and if, on the road, they did not move quick enough, they were urged forward at the point of the pike. When they reached the river, or the sea, they were precipitated into it in bands of several hundreds; which is, doubtless, an exaggeration. If these poor wretches rose to the surface of the water, men were stationed along the brink to plunge them in again with the butts of their muskets, or to fire at, and kill them. Husbands were cut to pieces in presence of their wives; wives and virgins were abused in the sight of their nearest relations; and infants of seven or eight years were hung before the eyes of their parents. Nay, the Irish even went so far as to teach their own children to strip and kill the children of the English, and dash out their brains against the stones. Numbers of Protestants were buried alive — as many as seventy in one trench."

Burning under wrongs like these, Cromwell had been sweeping through unhappy Ireland, and now had arrived at Drogheda, and on the 3d of Sept., 1649, was encamped before the walls. The famous and brave Ormond had planted behind those walls his heaviest cannon and his choicest soldiers, and deemed his position impregnable. For six days did Cromwell labor to fortify the neighboring hills, and when all was ready, his red flag was hoisted, and his iron rain began to fall upon the city. You know the historic facts; the siege continued until

Drogheda was one vast pile of ruins, one common receptacle of death. The streets ran with blood; the doomed people cried for mercy in vain; hundreds were driven into a wooden church, which was set on fire, and they were consumed; and in ancient or modern warfare scarcely an instance can be found to equal this terrible revenge. This scene rose before us as we walked those streets, once slippery with blood, and as we gazed upon the relics of that fearful siege.

But the next day we were obliged to leave, and taking a northward course, by where the famous battle of the Boyne was fought, by the very spot whereon the tent of the King was pitched, where he watched the battle, to Belfast, in the distant North. Belfast is called "The Athens of Ireland," and is a very fine place. We visited the public places: the "Queen's College," the new "Custom-house," and "Stamp-office," and various public buildings. But we spent the most time around the manufactories, going through, and spending hours in the works of the "York Street Flax-Spinning Company." This establishment, for the manufacture of linen, employs three hundred men, and twelve hundred females. The latter, from children of twelve to women of fifty, were barefoot, very few had shoes on. The floors were of brick, cold, oily, and damp. I could but contrast this manufactory with those I had been accustomed to see in America, where neatness and even gentility are found. The process of flax-manufacture would not be new to you, and I need not describe it.

I have thus selected three Irish towns to give three phases of Irish life, — Dublin, the capital; Drogheda, where the old Irish church is found unchanged; and Belfast, a literary city, where high intelligence mingles with growing industry. We saw other spots in Ireland, but as my time has expired, I must pass them by without notice. My recollections of Ireland are most happy. Naturally, it is one of the most beautiful and fertile countries on the earth. As we passed through Dunleer, Dundalk, Portadown, and other places, the whole country seemed to be alive with industry and fertility. The lowest valleys and the highest hills were alike glowing with the richness of the season. No wonder the Irishman is so proud of the land which gave him birth. Perhaps it would not be unjust to say that the Irishman, as seen in America, is not the type of the Irishman seen in Ireland. With some exceptions, the poorer classes go to the United States, and they are not fair specimens of what are left behind.

Having seen enough of the country to obtain a tolerable idea of its resources, scenery, and people, I went down to the pier, and took the steamer for Glasgow; and, as I bid you good-night, you may imagine me standing on the deck of the little steamer "Reindeer," which is to bear me over to Scotland, to which country I shall ask you to accompany me at the next meeting of the "Triangle."

RIP VAN WINKLE.

IN SCOTLAND.

THE CLYDE, NEAR COULTER.

THE interest excited by the first letter of Rip Van Winkle led the Triangle to expect the next with the utmost anxiety. The days did not fly away fast enough. But before the time came for the arrival of the letter, it was decided that a few friends should be invited. The day at length arrived, and the letter. Hal brought his two sisters; Will came with two boys a little older than himself; while Charlie, being president, had taken the liberty to bring two young men and two young ladies. The visitors gave *éclât* to the occasion, and the members of the club were conscious of maintaining the dignity of the organization. Charlie struck the table with his gavel and called the club to order. Hal read the records. Will moved that distinguished strangers present be invited to debate on all subjects and vote on none. Charlie put the question, and Hal voted it—unanimously. Then the correspondence of Master Van Wert was opened.

"Give silence all," said the president, "while the budget of our travelling correspondent is opened, and the contents read." The seal was broken, and the well-known handwriting of Rip Van Winkle was seen, and this is what he wrote:

GLASGOW.

Early morning found us in the river Clyde, on our way to this clean and beautiful city. Going up we touched at Greenock, and passed Newark and Dumbarton Castles, so picturesquely situated on the river, and reached the city just as the bright morning sun began to pour its broad beams upon the earth. I had my mind made up about Glasgow. I thought it was the Liverpool of Scotland, a commercial city, filled up with sailors and laboring men, and subject to changes and fluctuations, which made it undesirable as a residence, and of no great interest to the traveller.

But I soon found that I had mistaken the place entirely, that my idea of it was erroneous altogether; for instead of being a confused and inelegant city it was one of the finest I had ever seen. The houses and stores are elegant, the parks well laid out and finely cared for, the streets wide and clean, and the whole city having an elegance for which I was wholly unprepared.

After taking breakfast, we drove out to the Necropolis, one of the most finely located cemeteries I ever saw. It is situated on the side of a high hill, and separated from the city by a deep ravine, which is crossed by a fine bridge. The monuments rise one above the other, the hill being terraced to the summit. Nothing could be finer than the first view of this charming spot. At a single glance the whole ground is seen; the monuments and garniture of the place are all spread out to the eye in one magnificent slope of beauty. We crossed the bridge, and by winding paths reached the summit, and were greeted with a glorious view of the country for many miles around.

In the centre of the cemetery, and most conspicuous among the works of art found here, is a high pillar, surmounted by a colossal statue of that true-hearted old reformer, John Knox, whose power at the Throne of Grace made popish Queen Mary say that she "feared the prayers of John Knox more than all the armies of England." Well she might, for the King to whom the reformer prayed had more power than all the armies of the world. The pedestal is about forty feet high, and on the top stands Knox. His cap is on his head, his gown enfolds his person, his long beard hangs upon his bosom, and you see the iron firmness written on every feature. The base of the pedestal is covered with inscriptions to the imperishable memory of men who sealed their devotion to truth with their lives.

Here, too, is the monument of John Dick, D.D., who died in 1833; also a very fine statue of William McGowen, a prominent Protestant merchant, and author of several Protestant works; also a fine monument to the memory of Charles Tenant, who died 1858. The venerable old man sits in his chair on a pedestal. Thus he died, and his sons reared this pile. Also a most elaborate and exquisite monument to John Henry Alexander, who died in 1851. It is one of the most finished pieces of sculpture of the kind in the world.

Many eminent men of all professions and ranks lie here, and their monuments look down upon the city below, as if to remind the people of the awful conquests of death. I dwell thus long upon this spot because of the beauty of its location and the honored dust which is here entombed.

From the Necropolis we went to the cathedral, which is at the foot of the hill, across the ravine. Entering the porter's lodge, we took a guide in handsome livery, who went in with us. This cathedral has been built at different periods, part having been added to part, at intervals. The main edifice was built by Bishop Josceline, in 1408. The crypts in which some of the old Scottish kings lie entombed were built in 1490. Other parts of the building go back to an earlier date. The old well from which the priests and bishops drew the holy water was shown us; and we went into many dim old chapels which required no effort of imagination to make them look as if they were familiar with dark and horrid deeds. In visiting the public edifices, driving through the streets, wandering over the public parks, our time in Glasgow was spent. The beauty of the houses in the court end of the city, the public squares there laid out, the noble churches there erected, gave me a most delightful idea of the place.

DOUGLAS CASTLE.

EDINBURGH.

Leaving Glasgow, we hurried to Edinburgh, about two hours' ride distant, where we spent several days. Edinburgh is a peculiar, yet a very noble city. It has an old town and a new town, lying on each side of a deep ravine, the bed of which is occupied with railroad tracks and dépôts. You have only to picture to yourself a deep valley, with long ridges on each side. On the south side is the old town, with its houses rising up six, eight, and ten stories; its venerable old churches, its narrow, crooked streets, its impoverished inhabitants, its squalid wretchedness; and on the other side, occupying the slope of the hill, the new town, with its wide streets, well laid out parks, costly church edifices, noble public buildings, and fashionable people. Opposite to each other, on the right and left banks of the ravine, the two towns slope towards each other, one the representative of the past, with its dim old memories, and the other the representative of the present, with its improvements and conveniences, its luxuries and elegancies.

There is much in Edinburgh to interest and please a stranger, especially an American. Among them is the cemetery where repose the ashes of the noble old covenanters. Several hospitals, among them one for poor children, founded by James Donaldson, who left for this purpose about one million of dollars. It accommodates three hundred children. The building was erected at an enormous expense. Also one erected and endowed by George Heriot, for fatherless boys, and many other noble institutions of the same kind, which owe their existence to private munificence. There are in Edinburgh many private houses of note, none more so than the building known as the home of John Knox, in High Street. I have said to you that Edinburgh lies on two sides of a ravine, the old town being on one side, and the new town on the other. On the new town side runs parallel with the valley a noble street — the Broadway of the new town; on the old town side is a long, crowded street, — filled with churches and stores, and houses of six, and even ten stories, — irregular, and full of people, running the whole length of the city on that side. In this street, which in old times was the main thoroughfare of Edinburgh, is Knox House. The sleeping-room and study of the reformer are still shown for a trifling fee. On the outside of the house, near the window from which he used to harangue the people, is an effigy of Knox in the pulpit, done in stone. On one of the outside walls is an inscription, "Love God above all, and your neighbor as thyself." There is also a stone set in the front of the house bearing the name of Jehovah in English, Latin, and Greek. In this old house lived a man whose name shook thrones, and whose dead hand, yet reaching from the old churchyard of St. Giles, holds the conscience of that religious people.

And as one wanders about the city, he will be pointed to several houses of much historic interest: one in which Cromwell tarried in 1648; one in which Lord Monboddo and the "fair Burnet," his daughter, immortalized in the stanzas of Burns, resided; and many others noted for events which have been used to deepen the plot of the novelist, or lend wings of flame to the orator and poet. Just outside the city is the site of the cottage where lived old David Deans, and Jeanie and Effie, all of whom figure so terribly in the "Heart of Midlothian." In wandering about Edinburgh, you find many streets mentioned as "Canongate," "Cowgate," &c., also you read of "closes," such as "Sellar's Close," "Craig's Close," "Flesh Market Close," and the like. These gates are streets, deriving their names from some ancient gate which long since has passed away. The closes are long narrow alleys running from the public streets, and are densely filled with people. From High Street several of these closes proceed. They are from five to twelve feet in width, and the houses run up seven or eight stories high, and each story is crowded with families. It is a curious sight, on a fine day, to walk through High Street just as the sun goes down. The people have done work, swallowed their hasty supper, and are pouring out into the street, shoeless, hatless, bonnetless — men, women, and children, all talking, all earnest. The street, as far as you can see, is a mass of heads; carriages are obstructed, foot-passengers find it difficult to get through; and the spectacle is one to be witnessed in no other city of the globe. The contrast between this narrow, long, densely filled street and rich, aristocratic Princes Street, on the other side of the valley, is marked and striking. There all is quiet, save when gilded carriages drive along, or richly dressed ladies sweep the noble pavements; and one who should take a view of the two streets would not imagine that they belonged to the same city or nation. For magnificence of location and beauty of public buildings, few cities can boast as much.

Our best glance at the city is from Sir Walter Scott's monument, on the slope towards the new town, which commands an extensive view of Edinburgh and its environs. This monument is two hundred feet six inches high; the foundation is fifty feet below the soil; two hundred and eighty-seven steps lead to the summit, and the cost of its erection was eighty thousand dollars. In a clear day the country for twenty miles around can be seen from its summit. As we stand there, two hundred feet above the ground, the people are seen surging along below: away in one direction is the castle, crowning a bare and rugged precipice; away in an opposite direction is Calton Hill; and still away in another direction are the famous Salisbury crags and Arthur's Seat. Nearer at hand are the Royal Institution, the Free Church College, Holyrood Palace, the churches, with old St. Giles like a mother among her children, and all around green parks dotting the landscape with great beauty. Away off in the distance are seen the rolling waters of the Frith of Forth, on one side, and the high houses of the old city, and on the other the aristocratic residences of the new city. Descending from the monument, we turn and give it a parting look. It is not a simple shaft rising in the air, but a neat, elaborate, Gothic edifice of red sandstone, with arches, pinnacles, carved work, and skilful facings, and many-formed finials. Within the structure is a statue of Sir Walter, who sits in his chair, while Scotland and the world come to pay homage to his lofty genius and splendid abilities.

Leaving the monument, we go out to Holyrood Palace. This old palace is a place of much historic interest. It was founded by King

David I. as an abbey, but in time became the residence of the Scottish kings. It is most noted for having been the town residence of Mary, the beautiful but unfortunate Queen of Scots. It was here that Mary was married to Lord Darnley, and here her secretary and probable lover, David Rizzio, was slain. Queen Mary was the daughter of Mary of Guise; her father she never saw. The stranger stands in Princes Street and looks down into the ravine before him, every spot of which seems a bed of flowers: he sweeps his eye around the horizon, and his gaze is interrupted by the old castle, the crown-like dome of St. Giles, the famous Arthur's Seat and Salisbury Crags, Calton Hill with its monuments and works of art,—and he takes in at once a panoramic view which is truly enchanting.

MELROSE.

We left Edinburgh, early one day, for Melrose, a name which will at once suggest pleasant associations. The country through which we rode was very lovely, but less so, we thought, than Ireland. Melrose is about two hours' ride from the capital, and is a small and pleasant town, surrounded by high hills, and beautifully picturesque. A comfortable inn, of the old style, just such as Sir Walter Scott writes about in his historical novels, furnished us with a home. Our room, at night, was an oaken-finished room, twenty-five by twenty feet, dim and dreary. The ceiling was eighteen feet high, and arched. Two beds, heavily hung with crimson drapery; a large table, with several candles on it; a large, old-fashioned sofa; the heavy red window-curtains, made it a strange abode for the night. The panelled walls looked as if they were furnished with sliding-doors, and the knock on them was hollow and echoing. One or two old portraits hung on the walls, and the eyes seemed to look down upon us from other days.

The sole object of the traveller in visiting this place is to see the old Abbey, one of the grandest ruins in the world. It was founded in 1636, and completed ten years afterward. About the beginning of the present century, an effort was made to repair it, and use it for a church, but the attempt was early abandoned. The roof is gone. The nave is two hundred and fifty-eight feet long, and seventy-nine high. The arches of the transept and the gorgeous pillars still remain. The Gothic windows, the doorways, and many other portions of the edifice are in a wonderful state of preservation.

I can give you no idea of this magnificent ruin, as we saw it,—the moss growing on the walls; the beautiful carved work rusted by the hand of time; the last rays of the setting sun streaming through the glass-less windows, all form a vision of mournful loveliness such as one seldom is permitted to witness. A bell and clock, put up more than fifty years ago, still remain, and at vesper-hour the bell sends out its peal. Beneath a stone the sacred heart of Bruce is said to lie. Douglass failed to carry it to Palestine, and tradition says it is here deposited. The Wizard's tomb, so familiar to the readers of Walter Scott, also meets the eye. Effigies of the departed heroes and ecclesiastics are numerous. Figures on the walls, within and without, peer at us, and seem to mutter from their stony lips. The light, airy stone-work is enchanting, and the delicate tracery seems to be the production of dreams rather than a reality standing out before us. As I looked up through the roofless arches, I thought of that truthful passage from the "Lay of the Last Minstrel":

> "The corbels were carved, grotesque and grim,
> And the pillars with clustered shafts so trim,
> With base and capitals flourished around,
> Seemed bundles of lances which garlands had bound."

We lingered long amid these scenes, a guide relating to us each legend connected with the edifice; and now, though weeks have rolled away, my thoughts go back to that shadowy place where the spirits of the dead seem to hover on noiseless wings. The time for visiting the ruins is the moonlight evening. That is the time Sir Walter Scott used to come, and draw inspiration from the scene. We saw it in the rays of the setting sun, and lingered there until gray evening threw her sombre shadow over the place.

We did what every stranger in Scotland should do, ascend into the far north to the regions of the famous lochs, and to the glorious scenery of the hill country. The wild scenery, the high hills, the grandly picturesque landscapes of Scotland are north of Edinburgh. One must go up and see the highlands, the regions of Rob Roy McGregor and the wild clans that, with a better age, have passed away. He must see Ben Lomond and Ben Nevis, and wander through that section where are

> "Crags, knolls, and mounds confusedly hurled
> The fragments of an earlier world;
> And mountains that, like giants, stand
> To sentinel enchanted land."

To get at the Scotch heart, you must go among the highlanders, who draw in the spirit of liberty with every breath. These hills have given to the world many a chivalric spirit, to say nothing of Wallace and Bruce, and the heroes who have immortalized their names on an enduring but bloody record. What a galaxy is presented to our view when we mention the names of Walter Scott, whose genius made the highlands famous; of Robert Burns, who sang the praises of his much loved isle; of John Knox, who shook the thrones of kings; of Chalmers, the leader of a second Reformation; of Pollok, whose "Course of Time" has been read in every land; and all that noble race that is still producing itself in such men as Hugh Miller, Peter Bayne, Wardlow, Cavendish, and a host of others. Edward Everett says that: "The throne and sceptre of England will crumble into dust like those of Scotland; Windsor Castle and Westminster Abbey will lie in ruins as poor and desolate as those of Scone and Iona, before the lords of Scottish song shall cease to reign in the hearts of men."

RIP VAN WINKLE.

IN ENGLAND.

OAKS AT BRADGATE.

THE next meeting of "The Triangle" was like the last, except that more strangers had been invited in, and a pleasant social interview took place before the real business of the evening was brought on. The piano-forte was brought into requisition, and music and song filled up an hour; and at its close, Charlie, with all the gravity of a judge, announced the letter from the Club's travelling correspondent.

NEWCASTLE.

I have been in England a few weeks, and literally journeying about from place to place, so I shall not give an account of the places in the order in which I visited them. As we rode down from Scotland, the beauty of England began to be seen; and but for the industries of the countries, — the shops, foundries, and manufactories which everywhere appear, — the country would seem like one great park, full of natural scenery of the most delightful variety.

Leaving the Scottish border line, crossing the Tweed, the traveller soon comes to Newcastle, a place famous for its coal mines and mining operations. The ride is along the shore of the German ocean, the waves of which almost splash upon the iron track over which we pass. Newcastle is a great city of two hundred thousand people, and to a stranger, a most disagreeable one. It was the blackest city I ever saw. We went in over the tops of the houses, the tracks in England not being laid on a level with the common roads. All the buildings appeared to be black with smoke, the streets were black with pulverized coal, and the faces of the people seemed to be begrimed with the dust and steam. A coal-mining town generally looks dismal. The clouds of black smoke which hang over it from January to December, begrime and soot the houses until the original color is lost, and streets, houses, churches, and fields all bear the same sombre hue. The whole region around Newcastle is a coal region. The very streets and houses of the town, and the fields for miles around, are undermined. The excavations run in all directions. The coal pits are very deep, and a descent is attended with some difficulty and danger. Some of them have scores of horses and ponies in them which never see the sunlight from year to year, and often the men do not come up from month to month. The ignorance of these miners is terrible. We were told by respectable persons that many of them are put into the pits so young that when they come to manhood they do not know their own names. They are called "Dick," or "Bob," or "Tom," or "Bill," and that is all the name they have. Coal is very cheap. The nut coal sells to those who cart it away, at about one shilling per ton. The furnace-size coal sells for a few shillings more. The nut coal is deemed almost worthless, and formerly was burnt in large quantities, to have it out of the way.

I said the first view of Newcastle was a *black* one. All around the city burned the lurid fires of a hundred collieries and foundries. Beneath us the black chimneys, on the black houses, located in the black streets, send up a black, dull, sooty smoke. The people, too, seemed to have just come up from the black regions under ground, where the damp, cold sweat drops from the walls, and the torch flickers on the perpetual darkness. The river Tyne runs through the place, but it does not wash the black stains away, but itself becomes defiled, and rolls on its inky tide to mingle with the purer waters of the sea.

A ride of four hours brought us to York, a place quite different from Newcastle. The streets, houses, and people all looked clean and neat, and an air of quietness reigned over everything. The hotel at which we stayed was as quiet as a village inn. York reminded me of the good old city of Salem; and as I walked out in the evening, I almost imagined I was moving amid the scenes of my youth. It has but a small population, and most of them are people of wealth and leisure; and one feels, as he walks along the streets, that he is in the midst of a people of refinement and luxury.

The chief object of distinction in York is the venerable minster or cathedral church. The last hour before retiring at midnight we spent in walking around this immense structure, in gazing upon its towers as the pale moonbeams fell upon them and gilded them with silvery light. You know this minster is one of the wonders of the world, and any description I can give of it will fail to do it justice, or convey to your minds any idea of its vastness and magnificence.

KX-ETEK.

THE GUILDHALL, EXETER.

It shows none of the signs of dilapidation peculiar to many of the buildings in all these old English cities. We wonder, with our Yankee tastes, why they are not pulled down, and more modern ones put in their places. At home we are accustomed to see every old structure disappear before the march of trade. Nothing seems sacred. Even Faneuil Hall and the old State House in Boston, and Independence Hall in Philadelphia, can hardly be kept from the hand of

Vandalism. But in England it is otherwise. There exists in the minds of the people a reverence for age, and venerable buildings are guarded rather than desecrated. The Guildhall shows its antiquity, and, instead of being pulled down, is allowed to stand, as an inhabitant of a past generation.

There are two little trips that must be made from London. Every one goes to Hampton Court and spends a day there. This is a palace on the Thames, a few miles from the city. It was once the palace of Cardinal Wolsey, from whom it passed to the government, and is one of the many residences of the royal family. For many years it has been a place of festivity and crime. Hanging in dusty silence, in the ancient halls, are more than one thousand portraits and pictures, and the connoisseur of art can spend weeks in viewing the works of the old masters. On these walls are the likenesses of some of the best and noblest, and some of the frailest and worst creatures that ever lived — indiscriminately mingled. Here is the portrait of Queen Catherine, consort of Charles II., who, broken-hearted by the irregularities of her husband, called him to her bedside to see her die after she was given up by her physicians, and so affected was he that he shed tears. These tears falling on her forehead, an evidence of unexpected kindness, gave a check to her disease, saved her life, and she outlived her husband twenty years. Here is the portrait of Lady Denham, who married at eighteen Sir John at the age of seventy-nine, and not loving the old man, and being detected by him in a love intrigue he poisoned her by mixing poison in her morning cup of chocolate. Here is the Duchess of Cleveland, of whom Bishop Burnet says: "She was a woman of great beauty, but enormously wicked, voluptuous, foolish and imperious." Here are all the queens, and prominent among them is Elizabeth at twelve, sixteen, thirty-six and sixty; a woman who often had her face painted, though it was destitute of beauty, and often distorted with passion. "A pale Roman nose," says

Horace Walpole, "a head of hair loaded with crowns, and powdered with diamonds, a vast ruff, a vaster fardingale, and a bushel of pearls, are the features by which everybody knows at once the pictures of Queen Elizabeth." If he had said as much as that when Elizabeth lived, he would have lost his head for it. And here, too, are many noble men, some of whom were killed on the battle-field, some assassinated, some poisoned by their wine, — a pastime that seems to be becoming somewhat favorite with the ladies in certain parts of the world in our day.

The gardens of Kensington Court are very extensive, and the walks are about three miles in extent. In the greenhouse is the largest grape-vine in the world, the stem being thirty-five inches in circumference; it bears every year three hundred bunches of grapes. In the garden is the famous maze, a piece of shrubbery, and walks so intricate, the paths crossing each other, that a person may enter and wander about within the area of a single acre for hours, without being able to find his way out. This establishment is supported by the English government, at an enormous expense, to gratify the royal family, who come here once or twice a year, and spend a day or two. It is the custom for her Majesty to give here every year a ball, not to her nobles and to the ambassadors of other nations, but to her servants and dependents. At such times all the restraints and dignity of the court are laid aside, and those who a day before or day afterward would not have dared to invite the members of the royal family, are as free and familiar as any of them. The queen at such times is accustomed to dance (or was in former years) with the gate-keeper, the vine-dresser, or the hostler, who may happen to ask for her hand; and the utmost freedom is enjoyed by all parties.

Another excursion made from London is to Windsor Castle, about twenty-two miles from London. This castle was built originally by William the Conqueror, and has been enlarged by successive monarchs until it is one of the most noble fortresses in the world. This castle was the favorite residence of Charles I. and Charles II., and the aggregate amount of money spent in its erection is $4,500,000. From its towers fine views of the country in all directions are obtained, and within are halls and saloons well worthy of royalty itself. The queen makes the castle a visit very frequently, sometimes spending weeks here, which she never does at Hampton Court.

EXETER CATHEDRAL FROM THE NORTH-WEST.

St. George's Chapel, where the church services are held, is an edifice which, for grandeur of architecture and solemnity of effect, is seldom equalled. In this structure is the famous cenotaph of the Princess Charlotte, one of the most exquisite and magnificent monumental statues in the world. Following a guide, one passes in succession through the chapel; the state apartments; the queen's audience-chamber; the Vandyck rooms, filled with fine pictures by that painter; the queen's drawing-room; the state ante-room; the grand vestibule; the Waterloo chamber, filled with portraits of the heroes of Waterloo; the grand reception room; the banquet hall; the grand church; the queen's presence chamber; and several others which I do not remember. This castle is also an expensive royal luxury, and is supported by the government, at an enormous cost; and yet the people love to have it so.

The cathedral towns of England are the resorts of strangers from all parts of the world, on account of the rare architectural adornments. York, Exeter, Lincoln and Chester, with many other places, are renowned for their ancient religious structures. The Exeter Cathedral is one of the finest of its order of architecture.

SHEFFIELD.

Doubtless the Triangle would like to have been with me in my wanderings through the manufacturing establishments of this place, renowned throughout the world for its fine cutlery. An investigation of a day or two was given to these workshops, which at one time had no competitors in this extensive branch of industry. You will remember, boys, that when you were children, about every piece of cutlery that came upon the table at home had stamped into it the words, "Rogers, cutlers to His Majesty." The founders of this great house have gone the way of all the earth; but the house yet lives, and the business is carried on in the old name. It would have been an eye-feast for you to have gone through this establishment with me, and seen the vast quantities of goods in this line which are on exhibition and for sale, from a perfect ten-bladed knife, one-half an inch long, to a mammoth pocket knife, with nearly two thousand blades. These knives are made to show the perfection of the mechanism, and well have the artizans accomplished the feat. One knife we saw had one hundred and twenty blades, and in the handle was a well-regulated clock. Another had eighteen hundred and fifty-eight blades, and one has been added for each year since. Then we were shown a knife more delicately made than that, which was on exhibition in New York, at the time of the fair in the Crystal Palace, with the most delicate "etchings" on the blades. There were views of London Tower, Westminster Abbey, and various buildings and cities in the old world; also, views of Albany, Troy, Washington, Philadelphia, and numerous other places in our country. The blades were about one foot long, and exquisitely finished. Having remained some time in this show-room, which is very extensive, we went into the manufactory. There we saw cutlery in the various stages of manufacture. Men in one place were forging the blades; there putting in the springs; there making the handles, boiling the horn, or filing the ivory; grinding, polishing, finishing and doing all the various parts of the work. The firm employ about one hundred and fifty men and boys, and a vast quantity of fine cutlery is turned out. To a mechanic a visit to Sheffield must be exceedingly interesting, and the few hours we spent amid those blazing foundries and smoking manufactories will not soon be forgotten.

From Sheffield we took cars for London; and as we shall be nearly six hours on the road, I will pause and give a description of the cars and railroad accommodations in the old countries. In some things the English railroads are superior to ours, and in some they are not. The roads are generally better built, and run above or beneath the common roads. Hence there are no disasters from crossings, and no cause for a slacking of speed. The number of men employed is very large, and all these men are most trustworthy. In our country a poor drunken fellow is often employed for switcher or flagman, because he will work cheap. But in England it is not so. Human life is held higher there than here, and if an accident occurs, the laws are most severe upon the railroad company. The station-houses — the French word *dépôt* is not used in England; and when you ask a man the way to the *dépôt*, in nine cases out of ten he will tell you he does not know, though he may be fireman or baggage-master; — the station-houses are much finer and better arranged than among us. The dépôt at Newcastle looks like a palace from a distance; its lofty colonnades, its magnificent outer gallery and its unique proportions, make it look more like an imperial residence than a mart of trade and the storehouse of industry. Within, its arrangements are perfect. No individual is allowed to cross the tracks. Each side of the rails is furnished with everything which can add to the convenience and luxury of the traveller: generous dining-rooms, equal in splendor to the dining-halls of the St. Nicholas Hotel; waiting-rooms with fine stuffed chairs and marble-top tables; attentive officials ready to answer any question or render any assistance; bookstalls where the traveller can find everything he wants in that line, from Jack the Giant-killer to Watts' Hymns, from Eugène Sue to the Bible; and every other accommodation which may be desired. There is no crowding, no pushing, no yelling hackmen; but the utmost order. No person can ride in the wrong car, blunder as much as he will; for, just before the cars start, the conductor comes along and looks at all the tickets, and if any one has taken the wrong car, he is set right.

As to baggage, there are the most excellent arrangements. If the traveller enters the depôt with his coat upon his arm, his umbrella in his hand, and his valise beside him, he can take each of those articles to a "Left Baggage Office," and have them checked, and be sure to receive them when he wants them; and a gentleman who has travelled in Europe extensively told me that it was impossible to lose anything in England, so systematized were all the arrangements.

The cars are not as good as our own. There are three classes of cars. The first class car is generally a short car, with two seats like a coach, the door in the side, and one seat in front and one behind. Each accommodates three or four persons. These cars are elegantly fitted, sumptuously stuffed and furnished, and one can sink down into them and go to sleep almost as comfortably as if he was at home upon his own bed. The cars will accommodate only six or eight persons.

LONDON.

We are now in the great heart of the British empire, the most awful city in the world. Elsewhere we find cathedrals, ruined moss-covered abbeys, and memorials of national history, mingled with smoky, crowded, manufacturing cities. Here we find the people of England. Here we see men. Here we find government, capital, influence, architecture, to a wonderful extent.

We had better go to St. Paul's Cathedral, and obtain a view of London from its dome. A stranger going into a large city had better at the outset obtain, if possible, from a high point, a bird's-eye view of the whole place, and then select objects of interest to visit afterward. St. Paul's is in the heart of London, and for miles the city is spread out around it in all directions. The cathedral, as it now stands, is a massive structure, designed by Sir Christopher Wren. It is a monument worthy of his genius. It was commenced in the year 1775, but was not entirely finished until about fifty years afterwards. Its entire length is five hundred feet, and it is one of the most noble buildings ever erected. The poet Montgomery speaks of it as

"The City Queen — this peerless mass
Of hallowed domes, and grey worn towers sublime."

The church is built in the form of a cross. The principal front is towards the west, and is thus described: "The main entrance is adorned with a rich and tasteful portico, the entablature of which represents the conversion of St. Paul, sculptured in bass-relief. On the apex of the pediment is a colossal figure of St. Paul, with two of equal size at each end, representing St. Peter and St. James; and along the summit of the front are similar statues of the four evangelists. The whole rests on an elevated base, the ascent to which is formed by twenty-two steps of black marble. The angles are surmounted by two elegant turrets, of a chaste and uniform character, each terminating in a dome ornamented with a huge gilt pineapple." Looking off in one direction, is seen the venerable Westminster Abbey — the sacred depository of England's honored dead. Within these walls the English monarchs are crowned. Here the head of Victoria was burdened with the bauble. But it is not the coronation splendor that gives renown to this building; but the silent dust that is gathered here, and the memorial tablets and monuments that adorn the walls and rise on every side. The stranger beholds inscriptions that carry him to every epoch of British history, and to every scene of British power and glory. He sees them in the sculptured stone, and reads them on the wall, remembering at each step the lines of the poet Rogers: —

> "Marble monuments are here displayed,
> Thronging the walls; and on the floor beneath
> Sepulchral stones appear, with emblems graven
> And foot-worn epitaphs; and some with small
> And shining effigies of brass inlaid."

The vast cost of this whole structure cannot be counted. The whole surface is rich with the wealth of time and art. The chapels connected with it, which are numerous, are exquisite in style and finish. That of Edward the Confessor, in whose tesselated shrine, enclosed in an iron-bound box, the bones yet are, is richly furnished, and kings and queens lie buried here. That of Henry VII. adjoins the east end of the abbey, and cost one million dollars, though it is but one hundred and fifteen feet long and eighty wide.

The statuary is rich in design and execution, and everywhere honored names appear to greet the traveller's eye. Here is Ben Jonson, the famous dramatist; and Edmund Spenser, whose "Fairy Queene" has not ceased to wield her wand; and tablets to Milton and Gray and Chaucer, and a host of other sons of song. Here are statesmen and warriors and noble men, whose deeds have been incorporated into the world's lengthened history. Ay, it is a memorable day in one's life when he visits this building and reads the names. The edifice itself is grand and imposing; but it is not that which makes the place awful. It is the associations, the memories, the histories that are written on the tombs.

> " Think how many royal bones,
> Sleep within these heaps of stones.
> Here they lie, had realms and lands,
> Who now want strength to lift their hands.
> Where, from their pulpit sealed with dust,
> They preach, ' In greatness is no trust ! '
> Here's an acre, sown indeed
> With the richest, royalest seed,
> That the earth did ere suck in,
> Since the first man died for sin."

I shall never forget how I felt when I first crossed the threshold, and stood alone in the centre of this awful pile. I seemed to have reached the confines of eternity, and to stand looking off from earth upon the vast land of the hereafter. I recollected what Coleridge, that great-souled man, said of his visit to the place: "On entering the cathedral, I am filled with devotion and awe; I am lost to the actualities that surround me, and my whole soul expands into the infinite; earth and air, nature and art, all swell up into eternity; and the only sensible impression left is, that I am nothing."

Near Westminster Abbey, are the new houses of parliament, gorgeous structures, worthy of the great English nation. The building stands on the site of the old houses of parliament which were built in 1834. There are two magnificent rooms, one for the Lords and the other for the Commons, these two houses resembling the American

Senate and House of Representatives, with halls and lobbies, porches and corridors.

In another direction is THE TOWER, founded by William the Conqueror. Here are kept the crown jewels of England, the crowns, the sacramental service used at coronations, with all the insignia of royalty. The Tower has a dark page in English history. It was here that Sir Thomas More came to his terrible end, his head having been struck off with an axe, while his daughter clung around his neck with all the heroism of childlike devotion. Here William Wallace was confined after his unfortunate attempt to give liberty to Scotland, and from here he was dragged at a horse's tail to Smithfield, and barbarously murdered. Here Henry VI. was assassinated — the object of foul conspiracies, the victim of unsatisfiable ambition. Here the young princes were smothered by the order of Richard III., in all the helplessness of childhood; and here the murderer afterwards met the fate he so richly deserved. Here Bishop Fisher was executed, to satisfy the malignity of a wicked monarch whose foolish pretensions he refused to acknowledge. Here Anne Boleyn met her fate, protesting that her only crime was in having lost the love of her husband, who, three days after her head was struck off, led the beautiful Jane Seymour to the unhallowed altar. Here the Countess of Salisbury, accused of treason, ran around the fatal block, the executioner striking at her head at every step, until she fell covered with wounds. Here Lady Jane Grey, the victim of the weak ambition of her friends, having suffered herself to be crowned, was confined, tried, and executed. Here Arabella Stuart was confined, until, her health departed, her reason fled, and covered with disease, she died a lunatic. Here the gifted Earl of Strafford was confined and put to death under the eye of Cromwell, soon followed to the block by Laud, the corrupt ecclesiastic and unprincipled statesman. Time will not allow me to dwell upon the scenes of horror which have here been witnessed.

In another direction is the British Museum, where the Triangle, if here, could stay a year, and not examine all that is treasured within its walls. In the ample spaces are collections of birds, from the tiny humming-bird to the bald eagle, from the goldfinch to the peacock; animals from the mouse to the elephant, the walrus, and the mastodon; human skeletons embedded in limestone; Egyptian remains in vast variety; mummies, some as they were brought from the land of mythology, others partly unrolled, and others entirely exposed. Every age and clime have sent contributions to this great collection, and here, daily, antiquarians, artists, and scholars come to study out the mysterious lines which are written on every feature of the past. The library connected with the Museum is the largest in the world. It contains more than one million volumes, ten thousand maps, thirty thousand manuscripts, and a great variety of seals, parchments, and papers. A large part of it was given to the British nation by George IV., and is well selected, possessing great value, independent of the number of volumes. Here are the original manuscripts of Tasso, Pope's Iliad, the works of rare Ben Jonson; also letters written by Napoleon, Catharine de' Medici, Peter the Great, Nelson, Mary, Queen of Scots, the various Kings of France, Washington, Bacon, Locke, Newton, Dryden, Addison, Franklin, Voltaire, Erasmus, Luther, Knox, Calvin, Cranmer, Latimer, Melancthon, Wolsey, Leibnitz, and others. One feels, as he gazes upon the autographs of great men, who have moved the world, some by the sword, and some by the tongue, and some by the pen, that he is communing with the buried past. His mind is borne back to other days, and he sweeps with Napoleon over the field of blood; shouts with Cromwell, "God and religion," as he rushes to the charge; stands with Luther before the Diet, and pleads nobly for the great rights of conscience; or sits down and gazes over the shoulder of Calvin as he composes the Institutes in his cheerless study in Geneva.

But I must not take more time in speaking of London. It is a city where one could stay for years and be finding something new all the time. Its churches, halls, streets, parks, all add interest or charms to the place, of which I shall have much to tell you when I return. Wherever I go I do not expect to find any city like " London — opulent, enlarged, and still increasing London."

BIRMINGHAM.

This is a great town of more than three hundred thousand inhabitants, distinguished for its extensive manufactories, its fine buildings,

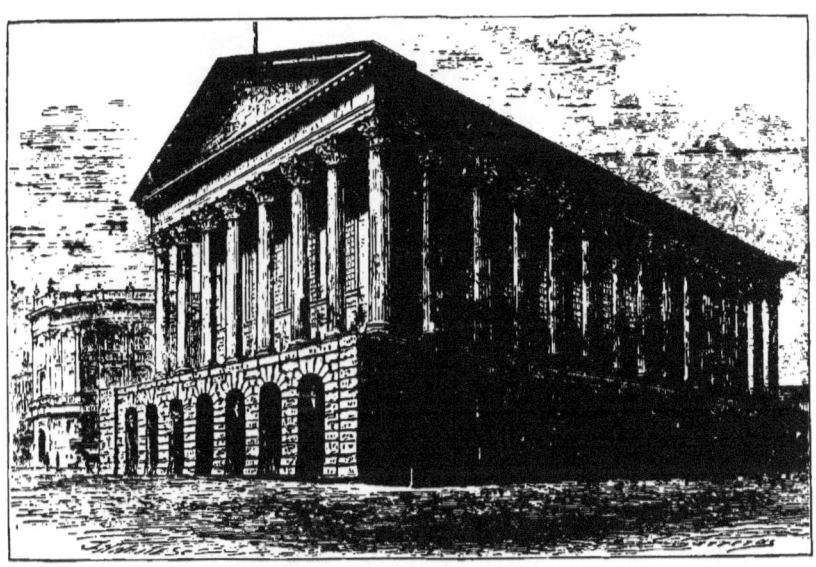

TOWN HALL, BIRMINGHAM.

and its thriving industries. The *papier maché* manufacturing, the electro-plate working, the steel-pen manufacturing, glass works, brass works, and iron works abound. Gillott's extensive steel-pen establishment is here.

The town hall is one of the most spacious rooms in England. It is built from the model of an ancient Grecian temple. It stands upon

a rough, coarse basement, on which rise beautiful marble co.umns, each weighing twenty-six tons, and being thirty-six feet high, forming one of the most beautiful exteriors seen in England. The hall is one hundred and forty-five feet long, sixty-five broad, and sixty-five high, making six hundred thousand cubic feet, and is capable of seating nearly five thousand persons, and standing an indefinite number of others.

In this hall is an immense organ, which is thus described by an inhabitant of Birmingham: " The organ case is forty feet wide, forty-five feet high, and seventeen feet deep. The largest wood pipe measures, in the interior, two hundred and twenty-four cubic feet. The bellows of the organ contains three hundred square feet of surface, and upwards of three tons' weight upon the bellows are required to give the necessary pressure. It is calculated that the trackers in the organ, if laid out in a straight line, would reach above five miles. There are seventy-eight draw-stops, four sets of keys, and above four thousand pipes. The weight of the instrument is about forty tons; it cost about four thousand pounds, and in the depth, power, variety, and sweetness of its tone, far surpasses any in Europe." This latter assertion is a matter of doubt, inasmuch as there are one or two others equal, if not superior, to this.

From the hall I found my way to the grammar-school founded by Edward VI., in 1552. The building used by this school is a fine Gothic edifice, of very elaborate design, quadrangular in form, with a front one hundred and seventy-four feet long, and was erected at a cost of about forty thousand pounds. The school is divided into two departments, one for the study of the English branches, and the other for the classics. The school was founded, and originally supported, by the income of a piece of land amounting to but thirty-one pounds. In consequence of improvements being made on and around it, the income has now increased to seven thousand pounds. About five hundred boys are here educated, without expense to their parents, by one principal and twelve or fifteen assistants. The principal received us with much courtesy, and conducted us through the various apartments. His salary is four hundred pounds. This school forms a most noble charity, and is one of the ornaments of that great city. There are four other schools, which, in a city of about two hundred and twenty thousand inhabitants, give instruction to about one thou-

COVENTRY—THE SPIRES OF TRINITY, ST. MICHAEL'S AND CHRIST CHURCH.

sand children, on the same foundation. I might take up more space in speaking of what we saw in Birmingham, but perhaps I have said enough to stimulate your curiosity. The city is quite attractive.

Nor does the stranger find the country surrounding Birmingham to be destitute of interest. Out at a little distance is Coventry, and the old ruins of Kenilworth Castle, and Warwick Castle and town, in which still remain the evidences of former greatness — the halls where kings and queens revelled in luxury. Still beyond is Stratford-on-Avon, the birthplace of William Shakespeare, with the old house in which he was born still standing. Still farther off is Dudley Castle, memorable in the history of the past, and living with the associations which link the past to the present and the future. Indeed, every inch

EXETER CATHEDRAL—THE WEST FRONT.

of ground in this vicinity is historic; every cliff, and hill, and vale bring to mind some scene of glory or shame of which poets have sung, or over which orators have grown eloquent.

EXETER.

I should like to have taken you with me to Exeter. To a person accustomed to the modern cities of the United States, a place like Exeter seems to be very ancient. A half century ago several of our most enterprising cities, such as Chicago, San Francisco, Milwaukee, and Denver, had no name on the map of our country. Boston, that at home seems so venerable, goes back but a little more than two hundred years. But here is a city that loses itself in the mists of the early ages. It is declared to have been a walled city before the

GATEWAY, JESUS COLLEGE.

advent of our Lord. How much back of that it goes no one can tell. The chief architectural feature of the city is its cathedral. Centuries of time have been beating upon it. It dates as far back as 1186. It is a monster in size, and a model in execution. I hope this brief allusion to it, and the view presented will lead you to obtain and read

that valuable and interesting volume, entitled the "Handbook of English Cathedrals."

We are struck everywhere with the evident antiquity. Cambridge and Oxford are the university cities of England, and in visits to them you would of course suppose that an old pedagogue like myself would take much interest; and many days I gave to those renowned places. The men who have gone out from those halls have stirred the world, controlled its destinies, and, under God, have moulded its future. At some time you will cross the ocean, and stand where I have stood, and muse on what I have mused, while spread out around you will be the classic treasuries of the kingdom.

ELSTOW CHURCH.

Another class of towns and cities I have visited, representing not the literature nor the industry of the nation, but its religion and philanthropy. Bristol is renowned as the theatre where Robert Hall won his laurels as the greatest preacher of his times, and where are the Faith Asylum Homes which are miracles of Christian love and labor. Bedford brings up the name and history of John Bunyan, the converted tinker, who, becoming a Baptist preacher, drew upon himself the persecution of his enemies, which resulted in his imprisonment. And this imprisonment gave to the world that wonderful book "The Pilgrim's Progress," which, next to the Bible, has done its work in guiding men to the celestial city. The history of John Bunyan, like the history of Joseph in Egypt, and that of St. John upon the isle of Patmos, is a striking illustration of that overruling Providence that marks out the paths of men, and directs the ways of this world to work the plans of Him who guides and governs all worlds. A statue of the prince of divines has recently been erected in Bedford. It represents Bunyan in the costume of his time, and is supposed to be faithful to the original.

STATUE OF BUNYAN.

Before I leave England I know you will want me to speak of the queen and the royal family, and will want me to give you my ideas of the nobility and gentry. In our country, where the poor mechanic believes himself to be as noble a man as the heir of wealth and fortune, in a country where all the avenues to wealth and greatness are open to the humblest citizen; where a bobbin-boy may be elected as the governor of a sovereign commonwealth, and a cobbler shine in the Federal Senate, among the sons of princely fortunes, and the graduates of highly endowed universities, we can hardly understand the earth-wide and sea-deep distinctions which exist between the nobility and the common people, on the other side of the ocean. The most sensible people pander to the foolish caste of birth and blood, and allow themselves to do homage to a man because he has titles, won in some cause of infamy, perhaps, by his dead sires, appended to his name. Nor can we understand how beggared lords and dissipated dukes put on airs when they met their less-favored fellow-creatures. In England the posts of honor, the high positions in the state and in the army, are generally, though not exclusively, occupied by the sons of the nobility; and this nobility is sometimes overbearing and dissipated.

The trouble grows out of the very structure of the government, and the blood of aristocracy runs from the queen on the throne, down through the meanest official that waits at her gates. In England, under a system of constitutional monarchy, the queen is only the representative of power, not the power itself. The Czar of Russia has power; the Emperor of Germany has power; in England the queen has but little. She cannot make a single law, and in the hands of her ministers and parliament is often a mere cipher. When the queen dies the Prince of Wales, who is now about forty years of age, having been born Nov. 9, 1841, will take the throne. But the government will go on just as well then in the hands of the son, as now under the excellent good-judgment of his mother. It seems strange how any people can be willing to be taxed so heavily to support a royal family — taxed on tea and coffee, on bread and butter, on paper and ink, on books and maps, on fire-wood and window-glass, to maintain the state of a family which, if it had been left to the election of the people, might never have been called to the throne. It must seem strange to the people to see such expenditures on one family, such homage to one woman, who, notwithstanding her virtues, is not superior to many of her countrywomen. You may, perhaps, have read, a few years ago, that the queen went upon a royal visit to Leeds, on the occasion of the opening of a large music hall. The mayor expended some fifteen thousand pounds, or seventy-five thousand dollars, to entertain his royal guest; but the lady mayoress not having been from the ranks of the nobility — the mayor in his marriage having consulted the impulses of his own noble heart, rather than the imperious laws of custom — her Majesty refused to speak with her, or notice her in any way whatever. The people of Leeds were indignant, and the public press did not hesitate to speak out the sentiments of the masses. The queen, perhaps convinced of her wrong, and solicitous for her standing in the eyes of the nation, sent the lady mayoress a golden bracelet, which the lady accepted as a sufficient apology. An American lady would have sent the bracelet back with becoming indignation.

And this reference to the queen leads me to speak of the palaces of England — the abodes of royalty. The town house of the queen is Buckingham Palace, a large and magnificent house built in the Mulberry Gardens by John Sheffield, Duke of Buckingham, from whom it derives its name. The present building has cost an immense sum of money, and constant changes are being made in it. Externally it is not an imposing structure, but within it is said to be a gorgeous abode. The state apartments, consisting of chamber, drawing-rooms, throne-room, and council-chamber, are shown when the queen is absent. As the best method of giving you an idea of the magnificence of royalty, I quote a description of the state rooms, as I find them particularized by another:—

"The Entrance Hall, though low, is truly magnificent; it is paved with variegated marble, bordered with a scroll of Sienna, centred with puce-colored rosettes; the walls are of scagliola, and the ceiling is supported by forty-four white marble columns with Corinthian capitals of Mosaic gold. Behind the hall is the sculpture gallery, extending the whole length of this portion of the palace, on each side of which are ranged busts of members of the royal family, and eminent deceased statesmen. The sides of the gallery are ornamented with thirty-two columns, similar to those in the Entrance Hall. In the centre is the door opening into the libraries, three handsome rooms, looking into the gardens; on the right is the staircase leading to the queen's private apartments; and on the left are the queen's study, and rooms for secretaries. On the left of the Entrance Hall is the grand staircase, recently decorated by Louis Grüner, the steps of which are of white marble, and the railings of mahogany and Mosaic gold, leading to the state apartments, which are in the following order:—

"The Green Drawing Room, forty-eight feet by thirty-five, is hung with rich damask drapery, with bullion fringe, divided by gilt pilasters. It contains portraits of the house of Hanover, and two valuable cabinets. Here every possible variety of green — from the deepest tint of that color, displayed in the striped satin by which the walls are lined and the gorgeous furniture covered — leads the eye up to the yellow of the gilt-work, by which the room is profusely ornamented.

"The Throne Room, sixty-five feet by thirty-five, is richly gilt, and hung with crimson silk, beautifully blended with an excess of richly gilt ornament; the ceiling is magnificently embossed, and the frieze contains bassi-relievi, by Baily, after designs by Stothard, representing the wars of York and Lancaster. In an alcove at the end of the apartment, formed by two wall pillars is the imperial throne, surmounted by a wreath, borne by winged figures, to which are attached a medallion, exhibiting the royal initials. In this apartment the meetings of the privy council are held.

"The Picture Gallery is one hundred and sixty-four feet by twenty-eight; and is lighted by three parallel ranges of sky-lights, decorated with tracery and eastern pendants, having a pleasing appearance; over the mantel-pieces are carved heads of the great masters of antiquity; and the floor is of panelled oak. The collection of pictures formed by George IV., consist principally of choice works of the Dutch and Flemish schools, a few valuable Italian paintings, and several meritorious pictures by modern English artists.

"The Yellow Drawing Room is forty-eight feet by thirty-five, and the most magnificent room in the palace; the whole of the furniture being elaborately carved, overlaid with dead and burnished gold, and covered with broad striped yellow satin. Against the walls are placed several highly-polished syenite marble pillars, which are matched in color by the carpet, subduing the effect of the masses of yellow. In each panel is painted a full-length portrait of some member of the royal family. There are also twelve bass-reliefs by the late William Pitts, representing the origin and progress of pleasure.

" The Saloon, which is in the centre of the garden front, is thirty-two feet by fifty-two. Here the decoration is particularly sumptuous; the shafts of the Corinthian columns and pilasters being of purple scagliola, in imitation of lapis lazuli; the entablature, cornice, and ceiling, profusely enriched; and all the other decorations and furniture, of corresponding magnificence. In this apartment are three friezes, also by Pitts, representing eloquence, pleasure, and harmony.

" The South Drawing Room is sixty-eight feet by thirty-five, enriched by columns of crimson scagliola, and three compositions in relief, by Pitts, being the apotheosis of Spenser, Shakespeare, and Milton.

" The last of the state rooms is the Dining Room, sixty-eight feet by thirty-five, which is a very spacious and handsome apartment, lighted by windows on one side only, opening into the garden, the spaces between which are filled with immense mirrors. The chief entrances are at the north end of the room; one opening from the ball-room, the other from the picture gallery, a fire-place, with an elegant looking-glass over it, dividing them. At the southern end is a deep recess, the extremity of which is nearly filled by a large looking-glass, in front of which, during state balls or dinners, the buffet of gold plate is arranged, producing a most magnificent effect. The ceiling is enriched with elaborately moulded foliage and floral ornaments. At the eastern side are portraits of former members of the royal family, and Sir T. Lawrence's celebrated portrait of George IV., in his coronation robes, formerly in the Presence Chamber, at St. James's.

" On the south side of the garden front is the private chapel, consecrated March 25, 1843, by the Archbishop of Canterbury. The pillars of this building formed a portion of the screen of Carlton Palace.

"In the garden is the queen's summer-house, adorned with frescos, illustrating Milton's Comus, by Eastlake, Maclise, Landseer, Dyce, Stanfield, Uwins, Leslie, and Ross; the poverty-stricken ornaments and border of which are by Louis Grüner."

This is a description of the state apartments. The private apartments of the royal family, which are almost numberless, are finished in a style of equal taste and splendor, all paid for by a people who, though beggared by taxes, throw up their arms, shouting, "God save the Queen!"

St. James's Palace, in Pall Mall, was the former residence of the royal family from 1697 to the accession of the present queen. It is now used mostly for the public parties and balls, for the queen's levees, and other similar purposes. Its external appearance is more like an almshouse than a palace, and within, its halls are gloomy and forbidding.

Marlborough House is the palace of the Prince of Wales, and until he comes to the throne, this will be his town residence, his city palace. It is in this house that the celebrated Turner collection of portraits was at one time placed, but they have since been removed to the National Gallery. Turner was the son of a barber, but his genius raised him above that condition, and he became an eminent painter. He left, at his death, a large fortune to be expended in founding asylums for unfortunate artists. He also bequeathed his collection of paintings, valued very highly, to the British nation. I have no time to dwell on any of these paintings, and a description might be of no interest to you. In the stable of this palace we saw the funeral car on which the Duke of Wellington was carried to the tomb.

I turn suddenly from royalty to the other extreme of London life. Indeed, one suggests the other, by way of contrast. I refer to the Ragged Schools of the city, a form of charity of which we can hardly speak too highly. They are unlike any schools we have in America;

either on week days or Sunday. They are generally located in the vilest and most loathsome parts of the city, among thieves and drunkards. One was established a short time ago in a thieves' lodging-house, called "The One Ton," a building well known to certain classes of people in the city. Like the "Old Brewery," in New York, it was turned into a mansion-house and a school established there, with four hundred scholars. The Field Lane school reformed the whole neighborhood, and changed that abode of theft and degradation into a very respectable locality. The Blue Gaté school also has done a great work in alleviating the wants and miseries of the wretched children in the east part of London. Nor is the good accomplished among the children only. One scholar in the Field Lane school told his teacher that he had been in prison many times for all kinds of crimes excepting murder, and that, on shipboard, he had been guilty of, but had never been brought to justice. I saw in this school a little lad, of whom the following statement, as taken from his lips, is recorded. The day I saw him he was about fourteen years old.

"I was passing the school on one occasion, and saw a lot of ragged boys going up to the school, and thought I would just go too. I have been in prison nineteen times; for stealing pencil-cases, box of cigars, gentleman's silver watch; for tossing pennies on Sunday; for stealing a lady's lever watch; for taking a coat out of a shop; for being in a house of ill-fame, where I assisted in stealing from a man, when he was asleep, his coat, trousers, and vest; for stealing a waist out of a shop, also a coat; for stealing harness off two horses; for stealing coat and trousers. I was taken up on suspicion of having taken them, but as no direct evidence could be brought against me, I was discharged. Since I have been out of prison, I have been stealing when I could; and I was planning a robbery when I met with the school."

One of the teachers of the Blue Gate school, in giving his report to the school, described a tramp that he had made through the more destitute parts of London, a few evenings before. He was in search of objects of charity. He first found a young man asleep. He was a man of color, and about twenty-six years of age. Being aroused from his slumbers, the poor fellow stated in reply to questions put, that he was a native of North America, a seaman by profession; he had come over in a vessel named the Macedonia; he had been paid off, but had foolishly spent all his money, and being penniless, and unable to get another ship, had taken to begging. He further stated that he had had but a very small quantity of food the previous day; but he did not so much mind that as having no shelter, nor place in which to lie down.

"Near the principal entrance of the London docks, about half-past one o'clock, I searched amongst some brick rubbish, which is generally deposited there, some sixty feet from the road. I climbed over the fence, and by the aid of my lamp discovered three human heads, just above the débris, the heads only being visible. I found them to be three boys, they having for warmth's sake literally buried their bodies, covering themselves over with old castaway mats, and heaped the rubbish upon them. The rain was then coming down fast. One was but fourteen years of age, named J. F.; he was without father or mother, and got his living, such as it was, by hanging about Billingsgate or Leadenhall Markets, and carrying parcels or goods. On market-days he might earn enough to pay for food and lodging, but on other days he never got enough for both, so he slept where he could. He declared he had only earned twopence-halfpenny the day before, with which he had bought two penny loaves which, with a drink of water, was his food for that day. The second was thirteen years of age, named J. K. He, too, was without father or mother, and lived by picking up rags and bones in the street; had picked up five farthings' worth the day before; and had not a friend in the world. The third was about twenty years of age. He had been parentless some time, and was a native of St. George's, and had resorted to begging and thieving for a living."

Next, he found a sailor, without money, asleep on the pavement. He had been drugged and robbed. Next, he found several men and women ranged along on the sidewalk of an alley, all asleep. Then, a little boy of ten years, who was nestled in against the wall of a sugar-house, which wall was warm and kept him from being chilled. Fifteen other similar cases he found that one night, all pitiable and distressing. Indeed, in London, in some of the viler and more degraded places, it is not uncommon, late at night, to see women sleeping on the ground, under the fences, or on the doorsteps of the houses; and it is this class that these ragged schools are designed to reach and bless.

We have now seen somewhat of London — its palaces, and its people. For want of time I have hurried over many things, and omitted others entirely. A man, to do any justice to London, either to its greatness, or to its vices and corruptions, must give a large volume, or a whole series of letters, to the subject.

England is a wonderful country, whether we consider its history, its people, or its influence upon the world, and especially is this so to an American, who regards it as " fatherland."

RIP VAN WINKLE.

IN FRANCE.

PALACE OF THE TROCADÉRO.

WHAT boy or girl old enough to read history, or become acquainted with the nations of the earth, who has not longed to see the city of Paris! There is a delightfulness about it that makes it the capital of gayety and fashion, — the headquarters of beauty and pleasure.

"Paris is France!" It cannot be said that New York or Washington is the United States, that London is England, or that St. Petersburg is Russia; but it can be said that "Paris is France." Paris is at once the head and heart of the whole country. Whatever is started in Paris is caught up all over the great country. It is not so in other lands. The capital plays a less conspicuous part, and has less to do with the districts beyond its own limits. New York looks down on Washington, Edinburgh on one side and Birmingham on the other snap their fingers at London, but Paris rules and sways the whole land. Its headship is acknowledged. And then Paris has a charm for young Americans. There is no country they like so well to read about or to visit as France; none that has for them so much delight as that gay and brilliant people, associated so intimately with fashion and folly as well as taste and heroism. So when the old traveller reached Paris he knew just what things to write about in his letters to the young friends at home. And when the letter came, the Club was more than usually anxious to invite in the older admirers of Master Van Wert. And this is what he says about France.

PARIS.

The first question I asked myself on reaching this city was, "Where shall I stop?" I find that the cost of living here is much greater than at any former time. But the question soon answered itself, and I was a guest at Hôtel Meurice, on the famous Rue de Rivoli. "I shall not starve here," I said to myself as one of the "bread venders" came into the court, laden with her daily supply. She was an interesting-looking girl of about twenty-five years of age. She seemed to have a whole baker's-shop on her person, the long loaves rising far above her head, as you will see in the little sketch which I send you.

And now we will go about the city. The streets are wide and clean. The Boulevards form very noble highways all around the city, and with them the most spacious streets of London bear no comparison. What the parks are to London, the public squares or "places," as they are called, which are generally ornamented with fountains or columns, are to Paris. Of the "places" and columns, there are several of much interest. The Place Vendôme is an octagonal space in which is the triumphal pillar erected by Napoleon to commemorate his German victories. The shaft is of stone, and covered with bronze bass-reliefs formed entirely of cannon taken in the battles of the conqueror. The bass-reliefs are spiral, and display the most noted events in the German campaigns. On the summit stands the bronze figure of Napoleon himself, who is looking out from his dizzy elevation upon the passing multitudes below. It is an imitation of the Trajan pillar at Rome, and surpasses it in grandeur, and in the heroism of the deeds which it commemorates.

In front of the Tuileries is the Place de la Concorde, ornamented with beautiful fountains which play ceaselessly, and in the centre of which rises the Luxor Obelisk, an Egyptian shaft, at least three thousand years old, and which is covered with unread Egyptian characters. It was brought from Egypt during the reign of Louis Philippe. On the base are engravings and diagrams of the machine by which it was raised to its present elevation. It is said that the engineer who had charge of the work felt the most extreme solicitude as to his success; and as thousands gathered to see the obelisk rise to its position, he moved among them with a charged pistol protruding from his vest, with which he had determined to commit suicide, if, by any accident, he should fail in his attempt. The obelisk stands where the guillotine stood in the time of the Revolution, and where the wretched Louis XVI. and Marie Antoinette, and their unfortunate friends, met a dreadful fate.

One of the best views of Paris is obtained from the beautiful cemetery, Père la Chaise. It was named for one who lived on the spot in the time of Louis XVI. The cemetery contains one hundred acres, and was laid out near the beginning of the present century. It

PARIS BREAD CARRIER.

was the first cemetery of the kind ever planned; and our beautiful Mt. Auburn, Forest Hills, Laurel Hill, and Greenwood are imitations of this. The ground is on an elevation which overlooks the city, and from its walks the edifices of the metropolis are all seen. The chief feature of the place is the numberless chapels, similar to some found at Greenwood, erected in the highest style of art. Here, in this cemetery, lie Abélard and Heloise, beneath a most beautiful group of marble statuary. The story of Abélard, his unfortunate love for the maiden, whom he should not have sought; the secret marriage; the subsequent persecutions, and the abandonment of both Abélard and Heloise to the degrading life of the convent, are matters of history. Our guide, a clever old fellow, about sixty years of age, told us that no one ever knew how to love until he read the correspondence of these two lovers.

Here lies Labédoyère, whose fate forms so dark a page in the records of French history, and whose only crime, says one, "was loyalty and faith sublime."

Here lies Marshal Ney, whom Napoleon so greatly and sadly wronged.

The grounds are filled with monumental chapels. A description of one of them will give a general idea of the whole. The one which I sketched was of soft sandstone, Corinthian architecture, seven feet long and four feet wide. A man could stand upright in it. The walls were thin, and the door of iron trellised-work, through which the interior could be seen. It was furnished with a chair, a prayer-book, several pots of geraniums, a vase of natural flowers, a kneeling statue, a silver crucifix, a miniature daguerreotype, a mourning picture, and some twenty-five wreaths of artificial flowers. A little table, on which some of these things stood, was covered with white muslin, and the floor neatly spread with painted carpet. In the rear, behind the altar or table, was a small stained-glass window; and the whole structure was neat and beautiful. The cemetery, with its hundred

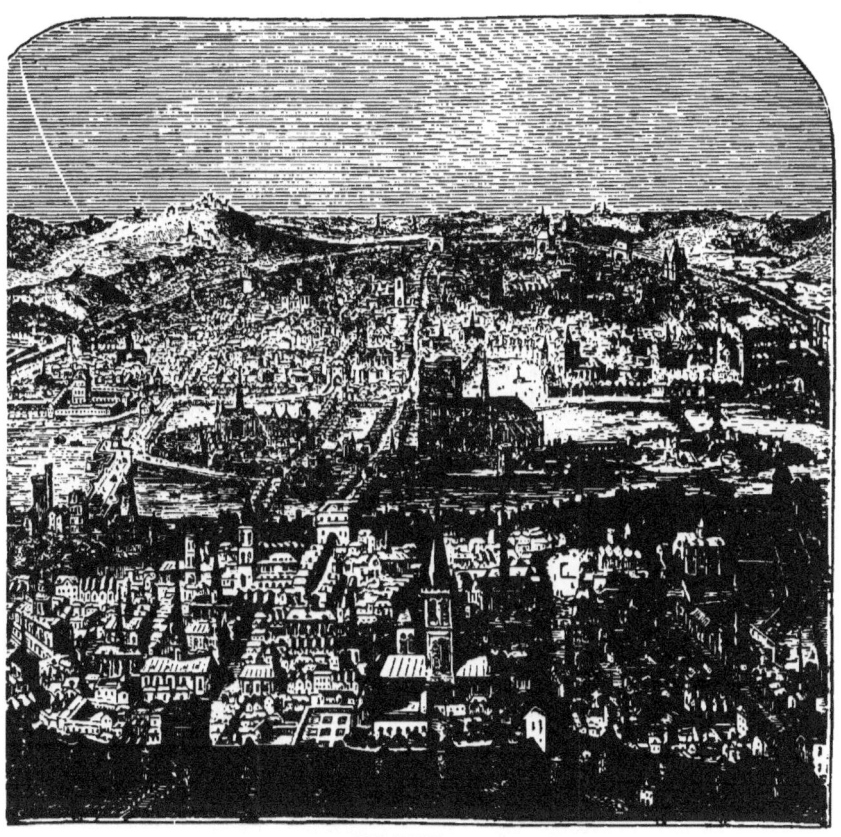

OLD PARIS.

acres, is filled up with chapels and monuments, beneath which sleep in death many who were once loved and honored in life.

Another fine view of the city is obtained from the Triumphal Arch, which is situated on high ground, commanding a wide prospect of the city and the surrounding country. It was begun by Napoleon, and stands as an imperishable monument of his genius. It was completed in 1836, and is one of the remarkable monuments of this city of monuments. It is like other works which originated in the brain of that wonderful "man of destiny." It was erected at a cost of upwards of ten millions of francs. One can spend hours on this high arch, looking over upon the beautiful city. No red tile roofs, no clouds of smoke, no dingy buildings are seen; but the bright, lively scenery of the French metropolis. The Champs Elysées thronged with people; the Place de la Concorde, with the churches, spires, domes and pillars of commemoration are all in view. The structure consists of a grand central arch, ninety feet high and forty-five feet wide, through which passes a traverse arch, scarcely less bold and magnificent in its proportions. The monument rises to a height of one hundred and fifty-two feet, and sinks its solid stone foundation twenty-five feet below the surface of the ground. The piers and entablature are richly ornamented with carved stone-work, and form one of the most magnificent triumphal arches in the world. The ascent is made by a flight of two hundred and sixty-one steps; and when, at the expense of weary limbs, the top is reached, one of the finest prospects conceivable bursts upon the sight.

One of the most conspicuous objects in Paris is the Church of Notre Dame, which stands on the site of an ancient Roman temple, and has resisted the assault of nearly ten centuries. It is one of the finest specimens of architectural taste I ever saw; but for the great purpose of worship, it is almost completely useless. Two towers surmount the structure, from which a fine view of Paris is obtained, in one of which is an enormous bell, weighing thirty-two thousand pounds, which sends out its iron tone like the voice of a giant. Decay and neglect are written all around, and the fine edifice gives many evidences of the ruthless assaults of civil war.

Many times I went into this venerable church. There is something which draws the traveller to it. One has an irresistible feeling of religious veneration as he stands beneath the arches of such a struc-

CATHEDRAL OF NOTRE DAME.

ture, where far above him the birds have built their nests, and the swallows are flying about with a mournful sound. In the chapels all around the church are paintings and statues, to commemorate distinguished events and personages. We were pointed to the spot on which Napoleon stood when he was married to Josephine by Pope

Pius VII. Here, too, was the spot where he placed the royal crown on his own head, and that of his imperial consort. What changes have befallen the Bonaparte family, and the imperial line since then. Little did the great Emperor dream of Elba and St. Helena; of Moscow and Waterloo. France has hardly had a peaceful hour since then. It has been revolution, bloodshed, overthrow and violent change. Whether this fickle, volatile people will ever go back from republicanism to monarchy no one can tell. They have tried all forms of government, and do not seem yet to be in a settled condition.

The Pantheon is a monumental home of the dead. Beneath it are vaults, in which is deposited the dust of some of the most noted men of France. The remains of Rousseau and Voltaire are here, — their mischief all done, and their specious errors all exploded. The famous Marat was entombed here; but the hand of revolution dug up his bones, which were thrown into a common sewer; and thus disappeared all that death left of a man whose name carried terror to a trembling nation. From the dome an extensive view of the city is obtained.

Of another style of architecture, unlike Notre Dame, or the Pantheon, is the Cathedral of St. Denis. It was once the Westminster Abbey of Paris, and in its vaults the French monarchs found their royal resting-place.

One of the most conspicuous buildings in Paris is the Hôtel des Invalides, where are quartered the poor and infirm soldiers who deserve well of their country. There, beneath the dome, was placed the dust of the Great Emperor, when it was brought back from St. Helena. The Hôtel was founded by Louis XIV., and is an architectural ornament and a practical charity.

Among the notable churches of modern date is the Madeleine, a costly and elegant structure, near the western termination of the Boulevards. It was commenced in 1796, and finished and dedicated during the reign of the last king. It is built in the Grecian style of

CATHEDRAL OF ST. DENIS.

architecture, and cost the immense sum of thirteen million and seventy-nine thousand francs, or more than two million six hundred thousand dollars. It is three hundred and twenty-eight feet long, and one hundred and thirty-eight feet wide. It is surrounded by Corinthian pillars about fifty feet high.

While the Catholic religion prevails in Paris the Protestants have several churches, the American chapel being well known and much attended by our countrymen. The Wesleyans, the Baptists, and several other Christian denominations have congregations which are more or less flourishing. The Religious Tract Society has a depôt where all the books of that and similar societies can be found, no hindrance being put upon the circulation of Protestant books.

The houses of Paris have a clean and inviting appearance. The light stone, of which so many are built, gives them an airy, pleasant aspect in wide contrast with the dingy brick of London. A visitor does not find so many dilapidated houses, or houses dating back to another age, as he might suppose he would. Paris has a modern look. There are structures that speak of great age; but they are not so numerous here as in other parts of France. In Lyons, Rouen, Valenciennes, old houses, halls and churches convey the traveller back to other ages and former days, in spite of himself.

In walking through Rue de Rivoli, the tall tower of St. Jacques meets the eye, a picturesque and striking monument of other days, intensely interesting to me, though not often mentioned by travellers.

The palaces of France have, with the departure of royalty, lost their former glory. A huge edifice, once the home of a king, but now the resort of artists, laborers, curiosity-seekers, poorly kept and much neglected, is a melancholy place. The Palais Royal, the early home of Louis XIV., built by Cardinal Richelieu and presented to the young monarch, is much neglected. The author of "Crests from the Ocean World" describes it as he saw it while it was the abode of Louis Philippe, into whose hands it came by inheritance: "A beau-

HOTEL DES INVALIDES.

tiful stairway to the first story, which is divided into three apartments, namely: those of the centre, occupied by the king and queen before 1830; the apartments of the left, appropriated to Madame Adelaide, the sister of the king; those of the right, destined for the prince royal. The left wing comprises a vast dining-room, several grand saloons, and beautiful cabinets. The centre includes the saloon for the aids-

OLD HOUSES, VALENCIENNES.

de-camp, that of reception, the cabinet of the king, the apartment of the queen, and the hall of the throne. A magnificent gallery, leading to the apartment of the late Duke of Orleans, occupies a part of the left wing. The library, situated on the same side, is placed partly in the entresol and partly in the first story. The walls of the several apartments were adorned with paintings, some of them possessing rare merit. Among the historical pieces were, Julius Cæsar going to

PARIS DÉPÔT OF THE RELIGIOUS TRACT SOCIETY.

the Senate, The Victory of Marathon, William Tell jumping out of the Boat with Gesler, and several more modern scenes in which Maria Theresa of Austria figures conspicuously. She is represented in attitudes expressive of strong emotion and intense energy. There are, besides, several portraits of distinguished personages; among them, those of Napoleon, Charles V., Madame de Staël, J. J. Rousseau, and the several members of the family of Louis Philippe. But what attracts more attention at the present time is the garden, with the exterior gallery of the palace. The beautiful enclosure formerly occupied a larger area than at present; as it comprehended, besides the present garden, the streets de Valois, de Montpensier, and de Beaujolais, as well as that space now occupied by the sides of the Palais, which have been more recently built. It was adorned with an alley of mulberry-trees, which alone cost Cardinal Richelieu sixty thousand dollars; but the old Revolution destroyed them. The place was once infamous for its gambling-houses, and the throngs of doubtful characters that swarmed in it of an evening; but the late government banished these, and the galleries are now occupied with brilliant cafés, and small, but magnificent bazaars. These are the fashionable shops of the city; and they are rich and beautiful beyond description. All that can tempt the luxurious, or please the vain; whatever can inspire admiration for the industry of man, for his exquisite taste; his creating genius; his skill in producing the elegant, the beautiful, the magnificent; in fine, whatever can delight the eye, captivate the senses, or add charms to beauty, are here displayed. One of these small shops rents for three or four thousand francs a year. The chairs alone, placed in the garden for the convenience of loungers, are said to give a revenue of eighty thousand francs. To see this enchanting spot in all its brilliancy you should go at night, when countless lamps pour floods of light through its delicious gardens and long arcades; when its walks are alive with gay promenaders, and its multitude of shops, cafés, and offices are in the full blaze of light, and gay people are coming in and going out, and people from many different climes are talking all together in strange tongues. There is nothing like it in New York, nor in any other American city, and the vivacity of these brilliant throngs is wonderfully exhilarating and pleasant to strangers. This is the time to see café life when in

TOWER OF ST. JACQUES, RUE DE RIVOLI.

the full tide of business. It is then, indeed, a scene resplendent with gayety, bustle, and animation."

The abodes of royalty outside of the city, such as St. Cloud, Versailles, and Fontainebleau, are in much better preservation, and more impressively remind us of the former kings and emperors than the city palaces, which have been sacked and desolated by revolut:ons. The scenes which have been witnessed in these places of pleasure and beauty come up fresh to the mind as we walk the paths and enter the groves. The Louvre, Luxembourg, the Tuileries, and other places once so attractive, have, under the Republic, been shorn of much of their former elegance.

There are two chapels in Paris of not great architectural attractiveness, but of tender private grief. One is the chapel of St. Ferdinand. It was erected to commemorate the death of the Duke of Orleans, who came to an untimely end in 1842. He was out riding in his carriage, when the horses became unmanageable; and, in endeavoring to leap to the ground, his foot was entangled, and being precipitated to the earth his skull was fractured. He was taken and carried into a grocery on the spot where the chapel now stands. His father, Louis Philippe, and the other members of the royal family were soon on the ground; but the unfortunate young man died in a few hours after. The old grocery was taken down, and a chapel, dedicated to St. Ferdinand, was erected on the spot. The chapel has seats for about fifty persons, and is fifty feet long, built in Gothic style. Opposite the doorway is the altar, and over it a statue of the Virgin and Child. On the left side of the chapel is another altar. On the right is a beautiful group of statuary, representing the prince on his death-bed, with an angel kneeling over him. This angel was the work of Princess Marie, the deceased sister of the duke, who little dreamed that she was fashioning the marble for the monumental tomb of her brother. Behind the altar is the little room in which the prince died, remaining nearly as at that

THE PARTERRE, FONTAINEBLEAU.

time. A few rough chairs, a confessional and crucifix, constitute the only furniture. On one side is a mournful picture representing the death-scene as it actually occurred. The duke is stretched upon a bed, pale and bleeding. The king holds his hands, with a countenance full of the deepest grief; the queen and many of the nobles are looking on or weeping in the most abject sorrow; while a robed priest, with a benign countenance, adds to the effect of the scene.

The other building of like interest with this is the Chapelle Expiatoire. It stands on the spot where the unfortunate Marie Antoinette was buried after her execution. It is in the little cemetery belonging to the Church of La Madeleine, and is an affecting memorial of one who was hated by the French people, because she was of the House of Austria. On the records of La Madeleine there still remains a charge like this: "*For the coffin of the widow Capet, seven francs;*" and this was the whole sum laid out for the interment of the gifted, beautiful, and high-born queen, whose word once made proud nobles tremble. With her husband, she was placed in an unhonored grave; and the ground was afterwards purchased by a stern royalist, who planted it as an orchard, that the traces of the graves might not lead to a discovery, fearing that, in some wild and terrible moment, the populace might dig up the bones, and insult even their decay. When monarchy was restored, the ground was purchased by government, and a neat chapel erected over the spot where the king and queen were interred. But I must take you outside of Paris. All over France are objects of interest and scenes of beauty which repay the tourist for the time spent in visiting them.

LYONS.

What Manchester is to England, Lyons is to France. It is the great manufacturing city, silk-working being one of the main branches of industry.

The city lies on both banks of the river Rhone, whose tide comes down swollen from the snows of the distant mountains. The streets

LYONS.

are clean and wide, and the houses are, in many instances, elaborate and beautiful. The people are divided, as is common in manufacturing cities, into employers and laborers, and as is usual there is a wide chasm between the two classes. The manufacturing establishm ıts are mainly on the outskirts of the city, and a transient visitor does n realize to what an extent they exist.

AVIGNON.

A wide contrast with Lyons does Avignon present. It is a dull, stupid place, and is famous for having been the French refuge for the popes, when they found it too hot for them to remain in their own capital.

AVIGNON.

I may have been unfortunate in my visit to this place, but it seemed to me to be one of the most uninteresting of all the French towns I have seen. There were more officious porters and hackmen at the landing, more officious landlords waiting to take advantage of our ignorance, more crying children in the streets, and more filthy, wretched habitations than I ever saw in any one place in so short a time; and of all the towns and cities which I visited, of but one other have I brought away an impression so unpleasant as of this. Other travellers speak very well of Avignon; but my impression was, that if half of the people could be shut up in the old popish palace, and the other half could be set to work cleaning the streets, it would be a passable town.

ROUEN.

Here the tourist finds himself in a city of the most delightful surprises. He visits Rouen without expecting much, but leaves it pleased with its churches, its shipping, and its venerable aspect.

This edifice is imposing within and without. The following just description of it, and the impression it makes upon the mind, was given by an American tourist some years ago, and will be true until

ST. OUEN, ROUEN.

St. Ouen crumbles to pieces, and goes to ruin: "We stand before the immense mass! The mind at first is almost overwhelmed with its vastness, its grandeur, its inexplicable power. The breadth is one hundred and three feet, while its length is no less than four hundred and thirty-four feet. Its elaborate and richly-ornamented front has three fine portals, over the central of which is a square tower, and a beautiful spire of iron-work, reaching to the dizzy height of four hundred and sixty-four feet eight inches, only thirty-eight feet less than that of the Pyramid of Cheops. This is flanked by two lofty but dissimilar towers. One of these towers, being older even than the remainder of the building itself, is in a simple and unadorned style; but the other, built at the end of the fifteenth century, is justly admired for the beauty of its architecture. As you gaze upon the complicated pile, amid the mazes of its inextricable details, your eye is lost among niches, corners, points and pinnacles, ornamented with images of apostles, saints, or, more frequently than either, of the Virgin and Child. These, however, are no unmeaning ornaments, but they served as a volume of religious history, conveying to the unlettered masses real facts of Scripture history, and fixed them in the minds of the people with a vividness and reality that could not have been secured so well in any other way.

"We will enter the gloomy Gothic structure. Our sensations admit of no description. It is not the religious sentiment which seizes the mind, only so far as that feeling is always inspired by the works of genius; but an indefinite and almost supernatural awe. The vast space, the silence that reigns within, the grandeur of the architecture, the solemnity of the monuments, the impressive power of the pictures, and the effect of all these objects immensely heightened by the light which comes streaming in from one hundred and thirty windows, the glass being stained with every shade of color, from fiery red to the soft tints fading into white, until nave, and choir, and aisles, seem magically illuminated; while they elevate the soul, — fill it with vague and profound impressions. Indeed, you leave the church, for the first time, with an oppressive feeling. The idea is too vast and complex to be received into the mind at once. We reach the sublime but by degrees; and it is only after a number of visits, and indefatigable studies, that the soul is expanded to anything like a just comprehension of the vast and magnificent proportions of the wonderful edifice.

Its contemplation awakens a new sphere of ideas. Its immense vaults within, enlarge the thoughts of man, — while the sublime works of genius around lend to it a spiritual glow and fervency, — and the summit, losing itself in the air, seems to bear the bright image of the soul direct to heaven."

Here, in Rouen, the heroic Maid of Orleans, "Joan of Arc," met her fate. She was put to death in the Place de la Pucelle, and a monument now marks the spot. It seems as if the people might have distinguished between heroism and sorcery, and spared this gifted maid for the sake of those brave deeds which have made her name an inheritance to her nation.

AMIENS.

There is not much to see at Amiens but the cathedral, and that will not be sought except by one who has given some attention to ecclesiastical architecture. Some cathedrals can be taken in at once. A single glance is sufficient. They strike the eye in their completeness. But like the Duomo of Milan, the Cathedral of Amiens needs to be studied. A lover of art can go to it again and again, and each time come away with a new conception of sublimity and taste.

France has here and there vestiges of the old Roman times —

Here some one of the visitors interrupted the reading with the question, "Did the Romans ever have possession of France?"

Charlie brought down his gavel and said: — "Will may answer that question, while Hal is resting." Will, thus called upon, did not know what to answer. He had not studied much in ancient history, but had a vague idea on the subject, and finally made a reply which was substantially correct.

"Yes, the Romans held possession of this country and Romanized it, planted their peculiar institutions and built their temples, some time before the birth of Christ. I have read of the passage of the Alps by Hannibal."

" Yes," said Hal, who had gone some further in his studies than the others, "the accounts of bloody wars for the possession of France or Gaul, are given by Cæsar in the 'Commentaries.'"

The gavel descended, and the reading was again ordered.

AMIENS CATHEDRAL.

France — says Rip Van Winkle — has here and there vestiges of the old Roman times. At Nîmes is an old Roman amphitheatre, which in its day would seat sixteen thousand spectators.

This structure is in a tolerable state of preservation, and resembles that class of buildings erected for the public shows of the times, of which the Coliseum at Rome is the largest and most prominent. Another will be found at Arles, an old Roman town, in the valley of the Rhone. It is not in as good a state of preservation as is the structure at Nimes. In various parts of France there are memorials of the old Roman warriors who overran the country and planted their institutions everywhere. The ages have made wonderful changes. The Cæsars

AMPHITHEATRE, NÎMES.

are gone; Rome has fallen; while on the sites of these old Roman cities is a more modern civilization, compared with which the best state and age of Rome were little less than barbarous.

MARSEILLES.

The jumping-off place of France! I came here to take the steamer on the blue Mediterranean, and found a bright, sunny, beautiful city, just like the French, gay and cheerful. I was pleased and amused with a visit made to the Church of "Our Lady," which stands on a rocky ledge overlooking the city on one side and the sea on the other. It is founded upon the ruins of a temple of the ancient Druids, and was built six hundred years ago It is small, dark, and dingy, and is evidently not designed for public worship. It is now full of votive offerings, which hang there as the evidences of a perverted religious sentiment. Sailors when in danger at sea, and men and women when sick at home, make vows to the Virgin, and when they recover, or are delivered from peril, whatever it may be, are accustomed to bring some offering to this chapel. These offerings are of small value, and have reference and allusion to the peculiar circumstances in which the person has been placed. Here are many pictures — some repre-

AMPHITHEATRE, ARLES.

senting a shipwreck, some a sick-bed, some one scene, and some another. They are in value from five cents to five dollars. Here also are models of ships; strings of beads; crosses; clothing which persons had on when saved from danger; crutches which were used by the lame before their recovery; wax and stone hands, feet and arms, contributed by persons who had lost such limbs, but whose health was restored. Some of these articles are very old, and some date as far down as the present year. On the chapel is a bell, beautifully chased without, and weighing twenty thousand pounds. The tongue is eight feet long, and must weigh near half a ton. From the

MONT ST. MICHEL.

NOTRE DAME DE LA GARDE, MARSEILLES.

flat tower of this chapel a fine view is obtained. On one side is the town, with its red-tile roofs, public buildings, churches, and its narrow, winding streets; beyond, imbosomed in rich foliage and shady trees, are scattered on the hill-sides six thousand country-seats of the more wealthy people; and behind all are the bleared and cloud-capped mountains. On the other side is seen the beautiful Mediterranean: first, the docks, old and new; then the harbor, in which is the island containing the prison in which Mirabeau was confined in his youth by his austere parent, which confinement made him the cruel man that he became. Beyond stretches the boundless blue, and we were told that on every clear day we could see out forty miles, which statement you may credit if you please. The harbor was covered with neat gondolas with fancy awnings, and lazy occupants lounging in the shade, while out to sea were seen the larger vessels, the full-rigged ship, and the puffing, bustling little steamers.

You need not suppose that I have told you all I saw in France, or have written to you about all the places which I visited. I have selected those places and objects that I thought might be most interesting to the Triangle. France is a beautiful country; with a more settled government, and sounder religious life, it would be the garden of the world. The poor people seem to be very comfortable. The women of the lower orders are cheerful and happy.

The French live much in the open air. In the city, they throng the public walks and gardens; and in the country, they cultivate the fields, and women perform much manual labor. I had often read of the part taken in the various revolutions by the women of Paris, but never could understand it. I had read of that mob of women which swept out to Versailles, and back again to Paris, controlling the army, overawing the populace, judging the king, and overturning the government, but was always at a loss to understand the secret. But a brief residence in Paris explains the whole. The lower class of women in France are accustomed to all kinds of hardship, and have unsexed themselves by the constant performance of rough out-of-door duties; and, by contact with coarse, uncouth men, they become as masculine, brazen, and bold as the soldiers in the army. Wandering through their pleasure-grounds, they present a gay and pleasing spectacle, with the sparkling black eye, and the frank, open countenance; but when aroused and maddened by revenge or want, enter into scenes of violence and strife.

The schools in France are not what they are in our country.

PEASANT AT HOME.

While there are some good schools, there are many poor ones, and in many parts of the country early education is much neglected. Whether France remains a Republic will depend on the honor and integrity of her people. There must be intelligence and patriotism, or a free government will not stand.

Rip Van Winkle.

A SCHOOL IN NORTHERN FRANCE.

IN ITALY.

THE CAPITOL.

"ORDER in the Triangle," cried the President. The disorder had been made by a score of young persons who had been invited in to listen to the monthly reading from the old master. The visitors were more numerous than usual, and more important. In one corner of the room, with his elbow on the table, was the minister of the parish-church where Master Van Wert, when at home, always worshipped. Centre of a group of young people, who were asking him all kinds of questions, was Dr. Oldschool, who had practised medicine for more than half a century. Besides these, several ladies and gentlemen had come in, to make the evening a merry one.

Order being restored, the communication of the honorary correspondent was opened. Master Van Wert first related the particulars of his voyage down the Mediterranean Sea, and gave an account of a visit to the city of Genoa, where the steamer anchored for twelve hours, giving her passengers time to see the city of Columbus. In all Catholic countries the churches are generally the chief objects of interest. They are the picture-galleries, the art-museums, and the

GENOA FROM THE HEIGHTS.

curiosity-shops of the people. This is especially so in Genoa, where the churches are numerous and superb, and are filled with all sorts of trumpery, from the bones of a dead dog to a marble Beelzebub. The old cathedral is built in alternate layers of black and white marble, and is an interesting though not a beautiful building. Here the superstitious Catholics claim to keep the bones of John the Baptist in a little chapel, under a marble sarcophagus. The bones are in an iron box, enclosed in another of marble. A great amount of money is raised upon these bones once a year, when they are taken out and a frolic held over them. In this cathedral is kept a dish, probably of glass, which the monks say is formed of a single emerald, called the *Sacra*

Catino. Some affirm that it was presented by the Queen of Sheba to Solomon; others declare that it was the dish in which the paschal lamb was put at the great feast; and others still assure us that it was the dish in which Joseph of Arimathea caught the flowing blood of Jesus as he hung upon the cross.

Continuing his way down the coast, the good master touched at Leghorn and Civita Vecchia, and at length reached the place of more interest than perhaps any other in Italy.

NAPLES.

Imagine, boys, that you have been dozing all night in the cabin of a little steamer on the Mediterranean Sea. Before your berth in that narrow saloon several men, not a word of whose language you could understand, have been engaged in gambling with cards and dice: now vociferating in the most villanous dialects, and anon rising with the most vehement gesticulations to clutch each other by the throat. Added to this, ten thousand fleas have taken possession of the cabin, and in legions are hopping about over the poor bodies of those who have been striving to get a little needful rest. Healthful sleep has been impossible, and you rise early and go on deck, to find the steamer just entering the beautiful bay of Naples. The full moon is just setting, and in the east the first beams of the morning sun are lighting up and reddening with beauty the horizon. Before you is a vision of loveliness, a panorama of beauty such as you have never seen before.

At first, perhaps, there may be a feeling of disappointment. The traveller, on entering St. Peter's at Rome, is always disappointed. Everything in that vast edifice is so well proportioned, the whole structure is so perfectly harmonious, that the full effect is not taken in at a single glance. It grows on you. You gaze and gaze, until a nameless awe creeps over you, and you stand dumb in the presence of that miracle of architecture.

So the bay of Naples is wonderfully harmonious. Sea and shore, plain and mountain, straight lines and curves, are so finely blended, that the stranger stands and gazes until his senses are absorbed, and his whole being is charmed with the wonderful beauty of this miracle of Nature! No wonder that the Italian enthusiast welcomes the stranger to his sunny land with the egotistic salutation, "See Naples and die!"

Into the bay of Naples you are sailing. The semi-circular sheet of water, covered with tiny boats, lies spread out around you. On one side, rising on its terraced hills, is the city of Naples, — its palaces, churches, convents, and gardens sloping to the shore. On the other side Mount Vesuvius, with its kindred elevations, rises full in view! "Is that Vesuvius?" the traveller asks, as he gazes on that modest-looking mountain, from which a stream of thin mist is constantly ascending. Who would think that so pretty a little hill could be capable of such acts of violence, such deeds of destruction, such monstrous outbursts of volcanic fury? Who would imagine that from that cone-like summit had poured forth burning lava, and molten stones, and heated ashes, enough in one night to bury out of sight, for eighteen hundred years, the most populous cities! Who could conceive of the fearful enginery, the colossal furnaces, the awful foundries, ever at work, down beneath that brown summit on which a light cloud seems to be resting!

We are on our way to visit that old mountain, to see the cities at its base. Let us stop a day in Naples and study the phenomena which prepare us for our explorations in Pompeii.

The whole region here is volcanic. Indeed, no one can tell how soon the city of Naples may disappear, and a burning crater occupy its place. There are evidences in all directions that smothered fires are burning underneath, and where they will break forth time only can tell. Vesuvius is now the great burning safety-valve, but if any occurrence should close that, these fires beneath would find vent somewhere.

One of the famous excursions for travellers, from Naples, is to *Baiæ*, the imperial resort, in the old days of Roman grandeur: an excursion which is almost startling, with its volcanic indications. The way out of the city is through the long tunnel, which Seneca called the "prison for slaves," known as the Grotto of Posilippo, a road dug out under a mountain, half a mile long, one hundred and fifty feet high, and wide enough for three carriages to drive abreast. It was hewn out at an immense expense of time and labor, and was probably the work of slaves; perhaps of the early Christians, who, incurring the displeasure of the pagans, were sent here to toil and die on the public road. The rock is volcanic, and was upheaved in some convulsion of Nature, the memory of which is lost in the lapse of time. Emerging from the grotto, the ride is through a country which bears various marks of volcanic influence. Hills have been cast up rudely by the wayside, and mountains overhang which look as if they had recently been disgorged from the bowels of the earth. The ruins of houses which have been shaken down by eruptions appear along the way, broken aqueducts and baths, and all the evidences of spoiled art and ruined luxury.

VESUVIUS.

The famous hot-springs, known as the "Baths of Nero," produce water so hot that eggs are boiled in it with ease in five minutes. They are ninety feet from the surface, reached by a winding passage, and a person bringing water from them reaches the open air covered with vapor and perspiration, and almost fainting with heat and exhaustion. One shudders at the idea that between a populous city, with its four hundred and twenty-five thousand inhabitants, and a yawning ocean of surging fire, there is but a thin crust, — so thin that at any time the pent-up heat may burst through.

Another reminder of what has been, and yet may be, is the little Lake Agnano, a sheet of water about three miles in circumference, situated near Pozzuoli. The lake is in the bed of an extinct and settled volcano, and the waters are very deep. At every eruption of Vesuvius, these waters rise and fall, showing a connection with the awful doings of that volcano, though it is between twenty and thirty miles distant.

On the shores of the lake are several grottoes, which are objects of considerable curiosity. One, the Cavern of Charon, now the "Dog Grotto," derives its name from the fact that dogs are here made the subject of a curious experiment. In this cave, a vapor rises from the ground which is fatal to life. A torch brought into contact with it is immediately extinguished, and a dog bound and thrown upon the ground will die in two minutes. The dog that was put in on the occasion of my visit remained about eighty seconds, and was, at the expiration, unable to rise. A pistol, loaded in the best manner, would not discharge itself when held near the ground.

Near by is an "Ammonia Grotto," or a cave in which ammonia gas rises from the ground. The earth is cold, and yet an intense heat arises from it; and, though no draught of wind can be perceived, one feels all the heat and gentle influence which are derived while standing over the register of a large furnace. The effect of inhaling the gas is highly exhilarating, and one would soon become intoxicated, as with opium or ether.

Turning from the volcanic indications found everywhere around Naples, we attend a moment to Vesuvius. This remarkable mountain, the destroyer of Pompeii, is about ten miles south-east of the city, its bleak grand summit rising to a height of three thousand nine hundred and fifty feet above the level of the sea. The first eruption of which we have any knowledge was that which destroyed Herculaneum, and since then there have been periods of hundreds of years when no great convulsion has taken place. Since 1631 the eruptions have been more frequent, and some of them of a character truly awful; that which occurred in 1779 is described as the grandest and most awful of these phenomena that ever occurred. The ashes that year were carried to Egypt in one direction, and to Constantinople in another. Stones of tons' weight were thrown into the air to a height of two thousand feet. One of the rocks projected from the mouth of the crater measured one hundred and eight feet in circumference, and was seventeen feet in height. In the eruption of 1794, a stream of lava issued from the mountain, estimated by scientific men to contain forty-six million cubic feet.

In August, A. D. 79, occurred the eruption which destroyed Pompeii. Early in that month the mountain gave signs of terrible activity. The lakes and ponds in the neighborhood were affected. They rose and fell without any assignable cause. Strange unearthly sounds, like the rumbling of a thousand chariots over hollow pavements, were heard. Now and then an opening chasm, emitting sulphurous clouds which hung like a sable pall over the doomed city, would be seen; and at intervals a jet of flame thrown into the air would fall just without the walls, as if the mighty powers below were trifling with the fears of men. The people were at their usual avocations, and while the volcano was preparing to bring its artillery to bear upon their habitations, they were shouting over the wounded, dying gladiator, and singing bacchanalian songs in the temples of their divinities.

But at length the hour came; and from the summit of the mountain flashed terrific lightnings, forked and fiery, and forth came a shower of ashes which darkened the sun; a torrent of water came down boiling upon the plains below, and a more fearful stream of molten matter, which directed its course towards the villages and towns which yesterday resounded with shouts and songs. The scene must have been one of indescribable and awful grandeur. That old mountain quaking and trembling, and belching forth huge masses of rocks and scoria, which, dashing against each other in the air, scattered into fragments, and falling upon the beautiful villas in the neighborhood, set them on fire; the streams of boiling water and sparkling cinders, mingling and falling heavily upon the house-tops and in the streets; the changing character of the whole scene, from lurid brightness now to dense and dismal darkness then; the long, hurried procession of slaves, with torches and treasures, hastening with their masters down to the sea; houses reeling and falling, crushing to pieces the fugitive in his wild flight; nobles and beggars alike asking for aid in vain; the wild outcries of the followers of Jesus, who imagined that the day of doom had come, and were uttering notes of warning; the pillage of houses vacated by their owners, by men who were unterrified by the convulsion of the world; and all the fearful phenomena of nature which that day were witnessed by the flying sensualists of Pompeii,—must have thrown over the whole an aspect of unutterable terror, equalled by nothing in the history of the world since the flood and the conflagration of Sodom.

You know that Caius Plinius Secundus, known as Pliny the Elder, a celebrated Roman writer, perished at the time Pompeii was destroyed. He was in command of the fleet, and his ship was in the bay of Naples. Wishing to observe the phenomena he approached too near the wrathful mountain and met his doom. Pliny the younger, the nephew and adopted son of this unfortunate man, in a letter to his friend Tacitus, gives an account of the sad disaster, and also the best account of the eruption extant. Speaking of his uncle, he says: "He was at the time, with the fleet under his command, at Misenum. On the 24th of August, about one in the afternoon, my mother desired him to observe a cloud which appeared of a very unusual size and shape. He had just returned from taking the benefit of the sun, and after bathing himself in cold water, and taking a slight repast, had retired to his study. He immediately arose, and went out upon an eminence, from whence he might more distinctly view this very uncommon appearance. It was not, at that distance, discernible from what mountain this cloud issued, but it was found afterwards to ascend from Mount Vesuvius. I cannot give a more exact description of its figure than by comparing it to that of a pine-tree; for it shot up to a great height in the form of a trunk, which extended itself at the top into a sort of branches, occasioned, I imagine, either by a sudden gust of air that impelled it, the force of which decreased as it advanced upwards, or the cloud itself, being pressed back again by its own weight, expanded in this manner. It appeared sometimes bright and sometimes dark and spotted, as it was more or less impregnated with earth and cinders. This extraordinary phenomenon excited my uncle's philosophical curiosity to take a nearer view of it. He ordered a light vessel to be got ready, and gave me the liberty, if I thought proper, to attend him. I rather chose to continue my studies; for, as it happened, he had given me an employment of that kind. As he was coming out of the house, he received a note from Rectina, the wife of Bassus, who was in the utmost alarm at the imminent danger which threatened her; for, her villa being situated at the foot of Mount Vesuvius, there was no way to escape but by sea. She earnestly entreated him, therefore, to come to her assistance. He accordingly changed his first design, and what he began with a philosophical he pursued with a heroical turn of mind. He ordered the galleys to put to sea, and went himself on board, with an intention of assisting not only Rectina, but several others; for the villas stand extremely thick upon that beautiful coast. When hastening to the place from whence others fled with the utmost terror, he steered his direct course to the point of danger, and with so much calmness and presence of mind, as to be able to make and dictate his observations upon the motion and figure of that dreadful scene. He was now so nigh the mountain that the cinders, which grew thicker and hotter the nearer he approached, fell into the ships, together with pumice-stones, and black pieces of burning rock. They were likewise in danger not only of being aground by the sudden retreat of the sea, but also from the vast fragments which rolled down from the mountain, and obstructed all the shore."

The account continues that Pliny and his friends and officers landed, deeming the earth less dangerous than the sea, and having advanced, with napkins upon their heads, near the mountain, he lay down upon the ground to rest, when, as his nephew states, "the flames and a strong smell of sulphur, which was the forerunner of them, dispersed the rest of the company, and obliged him to rise. He raised himself up, with the assistance of two of his servants, and instantly fell down dead—suffocated, as I conjecture, by some gross and noxious vapor, having always had weak lungs, and being frequently subject to a difficulty of breathing. As soon as it was light again, which was not till the third day after this melancholy accident, his body was found entire, and without any marks of violence upon it, exactly in the same posture that he fell, and looking more like a man asleep than dead."

Though overwhelmed in the same eruption, Herculaneum was destroyed by a tide of lava, while Pompeii was covered up by a shower of soft ashes. The former city was first discovered. King Charles of Spain fixed upon Portici as one of his royal residences. In sinking a well in 1738, three statues were found, which led to explorations, and these explorations being followed up, it was discovered that Portici was built above the ancient city of Herculaneum. Much interest was felt by the scientific world, but the labor and expense of excavation is such that little has been done to uncover the temples and palaces which are locked up in the rocky embrace. An old theatre, some works of art, certain ancient and yet undeciphered manuscripts, and sundry other evidences of a great city, have thus far rewarded the laboriou antiquarians; but no success that corresponds with the time, labor and expense of the undertaking. All future excavations made here will be slow and tedious, and meet with every obstacle from the inhabitants of Portici, who are very naturally averse

PERISTYLE OF THE HOUSE OF THE QUESTOR.

to having the town undermined, and its foundations hewn away. What lies beneath none can tell; what temples, what theatres, what exquisite works of art, what noble designs, what buried treasures, must long remain unknown. The work of destruction was not completed by one eruption. The stratified crustation shows that again and again the waves of fire have rolled over that doomed city, and the present quiet appearance of Vesuvius is no indication that lightnings will not again burst forth from its fiery bosom. The excavations now made only need a new earthquake to fill them up, and Portici only waits a new eruption to sweep its palaces away.

Pompeii being buried by a shower of ashes, the work of exhuming it has been more speedy and successful. Thus far about fifty acres have been dug over, and streets, dwellings, and public buildings are laid open. These ashes fell so fast that many had no opportunity to escape, or were buried in the streets as they were pursuing their way

BAKER'S OVEN, BREAD, AND FLOUR-MILLS.

to the distant sea. Thus far some three or four hundred skeletons have been found, while countless others may yet be lying in those parts of the city which have not been disinterred.

The impression made on the mind by a walk through the streets of Pompeii time can hardly efface. The pavements, the houses, the columns, as they were when, eighteen centuries ago, the torrent fell upon them, are on every side. The shops of the traders, with the signs still up; the frescoes on the walls, as bright and lively as ever;

the mosaics of stone and shell, clear and distinct; the various evidences of exquisite taste and finish, — all seem like a dream, when we are told that the hands that made them trembled in death before the crucifixion.

Entrance to Pompeii from Naples is by the famous Appian Way. At the gate you are reminded of the fact that, when the city was exhumed, the tall skeleton of a man in armor was found here. He was the Roman sentinel, and while others fled from the city he remained. True to his duty, he stood still while crowds swept by him out of the open gate. His own life was as precious to him as was the life of the most frightened refugee on that night of terror; but he was a soldier — a Roman soldier, who knew no word but "duty," loyal to no purpose but "obedience,"— and there he stood until death came, while the soft ashes closed around him, shut out the world, and left him standing for eighteen hundred years, a monument of fidelity and an example to all men.

Not far from where this soldier stood a group of four persons was found. A mother and her three children, unable to escape, fell down and died. She was found bent over them, her arms outspread, and her whole attitude indicative of an effort to save them. The world never reared a more significant monument of maternal love than that. It stood there eighteen hundred years — eighteen million years could not crumble it.

The story of Diomede has been told by Bulwer in one of his best novels. This rich man's residence was not far from the gate, on Via Appia. The remains show that it must have been a house of great elegance. It was probably, as it stood near the mountain, buried as soon as any other part of the city. When it was disinterred, the remains gave vivid witness of the last scene in the awful play. It is evident that the occupants of the house, finding themselves cut off from flight, or supposing that the storm of fire and ashes would soon abate, retired to the subterranean passages below, with lights and food,

GENERAL VIEW OF POMPEII

and wine, and there perished. Seventeen skeletons were found pent up in these vaults, whither they had fled for safety and protection— alas! their sepulchres. One of them was an infant, whose little form still clung in death to the bony bosom of her who gave it birth. Another was the little daughter of Diomede, the impression of whose rounded chest, made in the consolidated scoria, still is shown in Naples —the flesh consumed, but the bust remains to tell even the texture of the dress, as well as the finished beauty of the neck and arms. Two others were children, and when they were unburied, "some of their blond hair was still existent." In the common fear, the usual distinctions of life were forgotten, and the mistress and her slaves were huddled together, distinguished, seventeen centuries after, only by the jewelry which still hung upon the stiffened skeleton of the former.

Diomede himself evidently made an attempt to escape, but was not successful. He was found in his garden with a bunch of keys in his hand, and near by him a slave with some silver vases and several gold and silver coins. With what he could seize upon, the wealthy proprietor of the beautiful villa, attended by his trusty slave, left his family, who dared not follow him, and sought safety in flight, but only hastened his terrible end. His vast wealth, his humble slaves, his offices and honors were not respected by the descending fragments of stone, by some one of which he was smitten to the earth.

It was a custom in those days to punish men by fastening the feet in stocks. These stocks were generally in the highway near the gates, that the crowds constantly going in and out might see and take warning. Near one gate, two men were found thus fastened by their feet. The magistrates had sentenced them to remain there for a few hours—they have not moved for seventeen hundred years. When the shower began to fall, and the people to flee, the officers of justice forgot their victims, who were smothered as they sat wildly calling for aid.

The houses of the gentry in Pompeii were magnificent structures.

They were generally one story high, never more than two, but covered a large area of land. They consisted of suites of apartments on the four sides of a beautiful court. The rich pilasters and columns, the marble and mosaic pavements, the graven images, the frescoed walls, — all indicate an extreme of elegance and opulence. The house of Sallust is one of the most remarkable. Scientific men

ATRIUM OF HOUSE OF PANZA, RESTORED.

had no trouble in distinguishing it from others around it. The remarkable preservation of the frescos on the walls of this house show that the painters of Pompeii were acquainted with arts which are lost to us. We have no frescos now which will stand the assaults of time even under the most favorable circumstances, but these have resisted not only the streams of boiling water and the showers of ashes, but also the steady, onward march of ages, which with ceaseless tramp have been wandering over them.

The house of Panza is traced out, well arranged, spacious, and splendid even in its ruins. The doorway still remains, with its beautiful Corinthian pilasters; and the interior of the house, though broken and defaced, has many marks of its former elegance. The mosaics which yet remain, when the dust is removed from them, are found to be very beautiful, and show a carefulness of design and a correctness of finish which would do honor to the skill and taste of a later age.

The house of the tragic poet, so called, which was exhumed in 1824, is an object of great interest. The various apartments are full as the walls can hang with historical paintings. As the stranger crosses the marble threshold and enters the hall, a chained fox-dog, looking fiercely and preparing to spring, causes him almost to retreat in dismay. Farther on he sees various paintings, illustrating the customs and manners of the ancient inhabitants. The walls seem to speak forth eloquent words, and the longer one gazes, the more is he surprised at the accuracy of the work before him, and its wonderful preservation amid the changes of the past. Here is Jupiter wedding the unwilling Thetis to a mortal; the priests of Diana engaged in preparing for the human sacrifice; the great chariot-race between the gods; the battle of the Amazons; and many others. Many of these paintings are being removed to Naples, where they are visited by thousands, who gaze upon them with wonder.

The houses of the Great and Little Fountains, so called because fountains are the most prominent things found in them, and many others of persons known to have been residents of Pompeii at the time, are pointed out.

The shops are as interesting as the houses, and are more definite in their character. There yet remain some signs by which the different places of trade and the various warehouses are distinguished. Statues and paintings, illustrative of the different articles used, manufactured, or sold, and the different modes of operation, tell you where to find the shop of the baker and the house of the butcher. Three baker's shops have been uncovered, in which are the ovens ready for use, the mills in which the grain was broken, the kneading-troughs, the various articles used in the making of bread, and the bread itself, well done, since it has been baking so long over the fires of the volcano. The bread, of course, and the bakers' articles have been removed to Naples, and are on exhibition there. The loaves are flat, baked in moulds, and some of them are stamped with the name of the maker. They vary in size from six inches to twelve inches in diameter. The ashes in which they were burnt baked them to a crisp first, and then preserved them.

The shop of the apothecary, with all his implements, has been found in a tolerable state of preservation; and various other evidences of the trade of the city were found remaining when the excavations were made. These all show that the arts were more perfect in Italy, under the reign of the pagan emperors, than under the oppressive enactments of later rulers. The course of the people has been downward for centuries. The public mind has been enslaved, the public conscience has been seared, and the public hand has been palsied. The sweet voice of music, and the more rude sound of the hammer, have alike been hushed, and the noble faculties of the artisan were turned for ages to the construction of infernal machines, to rack humanity out of the children of God.

The Temple of Isis is one of the best preserved buildings in the city. It is eighty-four feet long and seventy-five feet broad, and now so perfect in its ruins that its construction and arrangement can be easily discovered. The private staircases, the secret tabernacles, the vestures and holy vessels, have been found. The altar on which the human sacrifice was burnt, and the oratory in which his bones and ashes were put, have come down to our times. Here in this temple, also, were found the evidences of the suddenness of the eruption. Near the main door was discovered a skeleton of one of the priests, drawn into the temple perhaps for plunder, and perhaps for devotion, at the awful hour when the city was being overwhelmed. The ashes, falling against the door outside, rendered his escape impossible. The posture in which he was found shows how terribly he

CLEARING A STREET.

struggled for life. A hatchet was in his hand, and on the walls, one of which he had beaten through, were marks where he had been endeavoring to cut his way out of prison, but in vain. The thick wall resisted all his efforts; the ashen rain fell faster; and the noxious gases, sifting into his narrow sepulchre, soon destroyed his life.

In another place, a priest was found sitting at the table eating. The remains of his dinner were before him. The remnant of an egg and the limb of a fowl tell us on what he was making his repast. Driven in from more public duties, he sat down to eat, thinking the storm would soon cease. Now and then, as he hummed a low tune, or breathed a superstitious prayer, he looked out upon the mountain that thundered, lightened, bellowed, and blazed full before him, and wondered what new display the gods were about to make. And there he sat, the room insensibly filling up with the vapor, which soon destroyed respiration; and, bowing his head upon his hand, he fell asleep, to wake no more. The temple was soon covered with the ashes, which, forcing their way into the room, made a winding-sheet for the victim.

In another room, a priest was found with a handful of coin, which he had probably stolen in the hour when fear prevailed in every breast. Stopping to count his treasure, or to look for more, he stopped too long; and, with the spoils in his hand, he died. Other priests were found, enabling us to conjecture, from the positions in which they were, that death came very unexpectedly, while they were attending to ordinary duties. Who they were, and how they felt, none can tell; but when ages had rolled away, they were found in the temple of their idolatry, victims at an altar where they had often caused human blood to flow in torrents.

Some one may ask — " How does the city as a whole appear? " Very much as one of our most beautiful modern cities would, if on some terrible night, it should be burned up, and destroyed suddenly by showers of ashes, stones, and lava, and after a while should be found with the roofs all broken in, the windows and doors gone or shattered, and the walls standing, with the stone fronts and fine columns, in many cases, uninjured. Something as one feels when he walks through a street the houses on both sides of which have been shaken down by a tornado, or swept by an extensive conflagration, leaving nothing but rocks and ruins, tenantless walls and crumbling remains, does he feel when pursuing his way through the streets of Pompeii. He does not wish to speak; the spirits of the past seem to be around him; he converses with forgotten ages, and leaves the spot saying, "I have seen a vision." Again and again does he turn back, gazing first on the destroyer, and then on the destroyed. Fancy again rebuilds the city, makes it active with life, and vocal with pleasure and industry. The Temple of Isis, of Jupiter, of Venus, the Forum, the Amphitheatre, the houses of the noble citizens, are all as they were ere the terrible overthrow. He looks upon the mountain, which, while he gazes, becomes agitated and troubled. Down its sides flow torrents of lava; from its summit, around which shadows and spectres dance, pour the shower of ashes and the tides of boiling water which fall on the city below. Consternation seizes the people. One loud, mighty cry — "To the sea! to the sea"— arises from priest and poet, gladiator and senator; and out they sweep, masters and slaves, leaving behind them houses and lands, and, in many cases, sick and aged friends. Still he gazes; but the people are gone, the mountain is quiet, and nought remains of Pompeii but forty acres of ruins and a vast pile of sepulchres, which are covered with the dust of nearly eighteen centuries. Only about one fourth of the city has been uncovered, and from the beginning the excavations have been slow and tedious. The great want of enterprise in this direction is unfortunate, as not an acre has been exposed to view without some substantial contribution to the science of archæology. The old Bourbon government of Naples was so limited in exchequer that it had no means for the prosecution of scientific discoveries, and the troubled state of the country for a long time prevented vigorous efforts to see what is still buried beneath the thick crustwork of ashes. Now

that the government of Italy is in Rome, and freedom makes the
Eternal City its capital, we may expect that not only Pompeii, but also
Herculaneum, will become objects of the greatest interest, and money
and means will be freely used in their exploration.

The streets which are now open run regularly, and are laid with
volcanic blocks of lava. They cross each other rectangularly, and
give evidence of having been laid out with scientific care. They are

SEARCHING FOR REMAINS.

quite narrow, varying from twelve to twenty feet, though there are one
or two from twenty-five to thirty feet. In all of them the carriage
ruts are seen deeply worn into the stone which, though soft when first
used, is now as hard as flint. Only the main thoroughfares seem to
have been laid out for carriages, or much travelling. As in other eastern cities, the business seems to have been confined to the great
arteries of traffic, while the minor streets were mere passages
between the various houses. Indeed, the street leading from Hercu-

laneum Gate to the Forum, which must have been much frequented, is only of an average width of twelve to fourteen feet. We must remember that in those days, carriages for private convenience, or for the removal of freight, were very few, and that travelling was accomplished generally on the backs of donkeys and mules. The streets of Pompeii are more spacious than are those of Constantinople or Cairo, at the present time, though they would be found singularly inconvenient in one of our own cities.

The city, as nearly as it can be traced, was oval in form, surrounded on all sides, except the part of the place which faces the sea, by a thick wall, which had in it formidable towers. The wall and towers must have been in a somewhat ruined state at the time of the eruption, as they show evidences of decay which could not have been wrought by the shower of ashes, and which are not found in the city habitations and stores. They had probably become useless, and had been allowed to go to decay.

The two-story houses were generally built partly of wood, the upper story being of that material. That story was not often used for living or sleeping purposes, but for storage and like uses. The soft ashes and cinders falling on them consumed the wood-work, and sifting down filled all the apartments below, preserving them, as they were found after seventeen hundred years.

The population of the city at the time was about twenty-five thousand. But few of these perished. The ashes, falling gradually, allowed time for the affrighted people to escape. Some who remained in fidelity to duty, some who were sick and unable to flee, and others who hid themselves, supposing the eruption would soon be over, seem to have been mainly, all that were destroyed. An irregular building near the great theatre, in which were found numerous war implements, also contained sixty-four skeletons, supposed to be soldiers who were too faithful to Roman discipline to escape. What the other portions of the city may reveal when it is uncovered we do not know, but thus far this is the largest number yet found in one place.

Probably the best portion of the city has been revealed. The Forum, in the south-west section, with its Doric colonnade, enclosing an area four hundred and eighty feet in length by one hundred and five feet in breadth; the temples of Jupiter, Venus, Fortune, Isis, Neptune; two theatres, the great tragic theatre, and one of less size, the Odeon; the public baths; the barracks of the soldiers, with many elegant private edifices are exhumed, and it is not probable that a city of twenty-five thousand inhabitants would have a much larger number, a greater variety of public buildings. Then nothing has yet been seen of any inferior houses, nothing to indicate a section for the poor, and of course those are yet to be found. It is most likely that the excavations commenced at the gate on the Appian way, struck at once into the best portion of the city, while that which remains to be uncovered will be of less interest to the superficial observer and the exploring antiquarian.

It is singular that for so many ages Pompeii should have remained undiscovered. It suddenly disappeared from history in August, A. D., 79. Until 1748—about seventeen hundred years—it remained undiscovered and unknown. Yet the average depth to which it was buried was only fifteen feet, and that too of soft ashes which a child could have shovelled away. An architect of note in Rome had commenced an aqueduct directly across it, in the early part of the seventeenth century, and about the same time one of the most distinguished geographers of the age had, after various experiments and extensive research, located Pompeii several miles from its actual site,—and all this while the highest buildings were protruding from the earth, beneath their feet. The covering of Pompeii must have been very slight. It now lies but fifteen feet beneath the surface, and it is likely that a part of this fifteen feet has been formed by subsequent eruptions. The crust seems to be in layers or strata, and these have doubtless been added during the lapse of seventeen hundred years.

Returning from Pompeii to Naples, the traveller always goes directly to the museum where the articles which have been taken from the excavated cities are deposited. There he finds bread from the ovens, drugs from the shop of the apothecary, household articles, and

STREET IN POMPEII.

many a beautiful mosaic or fresco, on which he gazes with wonder at its perfection, after having been covered up for so many centuries.

A description of Pompeii would not be complete without something in relation to the mountain which overwhelmed it. One of the most memorable days spent by the stranger in this region is that which takes him to the summit of Vesuvius. I may as well give my own experience, very briefly, in making the ascent. Some half dozen of us Americans started at midnight from Naples, designing to be upon the top at sunrise. Riding as far as Portici in carriages, we there exchanged that mode of conveyance for the backs of horses. At one we began to ascend very gradually, the road wide and winding, passing along by cultivated fields and rich orchards; but as we ascended higher these evidences of fertility were exchanged for dreadful sterility and death. The beds of lava were spread out all around us, and the desolation became more dreary every moment. We passed by the Hermitage and the Observatory, up into the more bleak fields, where not a green spot nor a single vine appears to relieve the eye or detract from the desolate scene. There are some places, however, on the sides of the mountain, where grows a vine of the grape of which a wine is made called *Lachryma Christi*, or the "Tears of Christ," which is said to be very delicious, and which is sold at a very high price. Up higher we ascended; our poor beasts picked out their way amid the fallen blocks of lava, now leaping across ravines, and then rubbing their sides against the torn and ragged masses, until the bridle became useless, and we gave ourselves up to the instincts of the animals on which we rode. About three hours after starting from Naples, we arrived at the base of the cone, and fastened our horses in the crater of an extinct volcano, or rather an older crater of the still trembling and fiery Vesuvius. And now commenced our toils. The cone is desperately steep, and we were obliged to clamber up over rough, rolling pieces of lava, which are set in motion as the foot treads upon them, and frequently three steps are taken backward where one is set forward. For a while, we toiled up the steep without assistance; but, at length, we called to several men trained to the work, who started with us from the base of the cone, and who handed us leather thongs, one end of which was fastened to their own shoulders. Accustomed to climbing, they moved on rapidly, and gave us much assistance. The tedious work lasted an hour, when we found ourselves at the summit, and standing on the verge of the terrible crater, just as the sun arose in all its beauty, and poured a flood of golden light over the mountain and the surrounding scenery.

At a distance, Vesuvius looks like a sugar-loaf, with a small, flat surface at the summit, from which a cloud of smoke is continually ascending. On reaching the apex, we find that what appears to be a level plain is a tunnel-shaped crater, with its yawning mouth about one-third of a mile across, and verging to a conical point in the centre. The morning was a very fine one for our view, as we stood on the east side, and looked across the crater towards the west, which was considerably higher. The ground under our feet was hot, and little crevices were emitting steam and smoke. The beds of sulphur, spread out all around, look pleasingly fearful; and the idea of the thin crust giving way, and letting the traveller down into the ever-churning vortex below, will enter the mind, and haunt it with forebodings of no very agreeable character. As we stood there on the verge of the crater, the deep below sent up its clouds of mist and steam, which now ascended toward heaven, and now hovering over the mountain, completely enveloped us in the sulphurous gases. We gazed down into the awful cavern from which has poured forth, in days agone, the desolating stream which has carried terror to defenceless homes and stricken hearts. The appearance of Vesuvius now is different from what it was when by it Pompeii was destroyed. It changes its form with every passing age, and spreads wider the barren covering upon the surrounding country. Strabo, in his time, speaks of the volcano as rising behind the beautiful cities on the shores of the sea, "well cultivated, and inhabited all around except its top, which was, for the most part, level, and entirely barren, ashy to the view, displaying cavernous hollows in cineritious rocks, which look as if they had been eaten in the fire, so that we may suppose this spot to have been a volcano formerly, with burning craters, but extinguished for want of fuel." But all is now changed, and the beautiful cities are destroyed, and the pleasant villas seem to be retreating from the mountain as if afraid of its volcanic fires.

Travellers generally manage to be on the summit at sunrise, and there breakfast. We did so; and cooked our eggs in the little ovens in the ground, scratching out a little place with the end of a cane.

It must be a wonderful sight to see that old mountain in one of its most fiery demonstrations. It must be worth a voyage to Italy to

THE GATE OF HERCULANEUM, AND STREET OF TOMBS, POMPEII.

gaze on this fountain of flame, blazing up to God, as if the earth itself was consuming. A writer in 1858, who saw the mount when in one of its troubled moods, says:—"It was a marvellous scene, that vast black valley, with its lake of fire at the bottom, its cone of fire on the top. The discharges were constant, and had something appalling in their sound. We were almost too much excited for observation. Now we looked at the cone of green and gold that sank and rose, faded and brightened, smoked or flamed; then at the seething lake;

then at the strange mountain of lava; then at the burning fissures that yawned around. There were yet some remnants of day; a gloomy twilight, at least, revealed the jagged rim of the valley. Down we went, down, down, to the very edge of the boiling caldron of melted lava, that rolled its huge waves towards the black shore, waves whose foam and spray were fire and flame! An eruption evidently was preparing, and soon, indeed, took place. We missed the sight; but what we saw was grand enough. A troop of heavy black clouds was hurrying athwart the sky, showing the stars ever and anon between, 'like a swarm of golden bees.' The wind roared and bellowed among the lava gullies, while the cone discharged its blocks of burning lava or its showers of red sparks, with a boom like that of a park of artillery."

The view from the summit of Vesuvius is one of the most beautiful in the world. The city and bay of Naples, the broad, blue Mediterranean Sea, the flowery enchantments of Italian scenery, fill up the vision. To stand on such a mountain, on the edge of that tremendous crater, marks the day in the history of a human life.

You have, perhaps, seen pictures of the descent from Vesuvius. That is quite a different thing from the ascent. The ascent is over sharp stones, that roll as you tread upon them, and the climbing is slow and tedious. The descent is on the other side of the mountain, and in seven minutes is undone what takes an hour to do. The traveller, convulsed with laughter, throws himself into a bed of fine cinders, descending nearly ten feet at a leap, sinking in the soft, flowing ashes, as if it were light, drifting snow, raising a cloud of dust, and setting the yielding body in motion all around.

How wonderful is this great system which God has made! In one place we see plains spread out in quiet beauty; then we see the immense masses of earth heaped together, and thrown into mountain ranges. Here we see rivers wending their way to the ocean, poetic as the Nile, historic as the Rhine, useful as the Thames, and beautiful as the Hudson; there we see the waters heaped up into liquid mountains and tumbling down like Niagara. In one place we have beautiful Lake Leman, and the hundred-isled Adriatic; and in another oceans in the air are turned to glaciers that glisten among the Alpine fortresses of crystal. But Vesuvius is different from them all. It is a monstrosity of nature. Man climbs its sides, and stands on the edge of its awful crater, with wonder and terror. It is so unlike every other object on which a human being can gaze, and so terrible, that he carries to the grave with him the acquaintance which he has formed with the rumbling, churning, smoking, storming pit, down into which no traveller has descended and returned again to tell the story of its fiery mines, which age after age burn on, supplied with fuel from the hand of God, and fanned by revolving systems.

And there they will continue to burn as age after age rolls away, and from time to time will flow forth the tide of fire, which will pour itself down upon the beautiful plains below, causing the inhabitants to fly in terror from the homes which they have decorated, and the graves over which they have wept, to find shelter and repose in villages beyond the reach of Vesuvius and its waves of ruin.

When the Triangle had finished this account of Vesuvius they spent the evening, until a late hour, in discussing it, and Dr. Oldschool, who was a well-read man, gave them much information concerning volcanoes and earthquakes, a subject which the letter had naturally suggested. An adjournment took place; and at the next meeting continued the narrative of the Master, as he approached the Eternal City.

In the city of Rome centres a marvellous interest. It was the capital of great Cæsar's Empire, it has had its long line of illustrious heroes, gifted orators, and celebrated artists. It is now the seat of one of the greatest religious systems that ever found place on earth. Here also are gathered wonderful treasures of art, and learning, and genius. Whatever is to be reverenced on account of its antiquity, is represented here, and few places on the globe can have more to attract a serious and thoughtful mind.

We reached Rome just at evening, crossing the Tiber by the Castle of St. Angelo, along the Corso, to a hotel where we were to stop during our stay. The city of Rome is built on seven hills: the Capitoline, on which stands the Capitol with its noble architecture and its commanding position; the Quirinal, still crowned by the noble ruins of the Temple of the Sun, built by Elagabalus, and beautified by the Colonna palace; the Palatine, on which Nero built his Golden House, the fame of the world, on the very spot where he had set fire to the city: the Esquiline, on which the Baths of Titus, an undistinguishable heap of ruins, lie shorn of their former beauty; the Viminal, which still bears up the remains of the splendid Baths of Diocletian, works reared by forty thousand Christians who toiled thereon, and where have been found bricks, on which, deep and indelible, is the mark of the cross, showing that even in their hateful slavery, the disciples did not forget their Lord, or the badge of their allegiance to him; the Aventine, on the eastern slope of which are the still almost perfect Baths of Caracalla, begun by him two hundred and two years after Christ, and finished by Alexander Severus some time afterward; the Cælian with its triumphal monuments, and its hoary ruins, — seven hills famous in poetry and song, each a theatre of wonders, and each bearing evidences of the genius and art that once abode upon them.

The city naturally divides itself into the Rome of the Cæsars and the Rome of the Popes. The stranger, standing on the summit of the Capitol, will see on one side of him old Rome, with its Forum, its arches, its pillars, and its ruins. On the other side he will see the living city, the masses of people, the modern buildings, and the Christian temples. Out on all sides, beyond these he will observe the desolate Campagna stretching away in the distance. Through the city and dividing it flows the Tiber, turbid and yellow, emblem of Rome herself.

We will look first at the Rome of the Cæsars — the city of the dead. We go first to the Roman Forum, a spot of ground raised about twenty feet, near the Capitoline. Once the resort of learning, the theatre of eloquence, the birthplace of liberty, it has degenerated into a place for the sale of cattle; and the confusion of tongues has taken the place of the eloquent strains of the orator. All around the Forum are the remains of the past: Temples in which the heathen gods were once worshipped, arches beneath which conquerors once rode, pillars erected to the memory of men whose deeds are now forgotten, and the remains of prisons, palaces, and other public edifices. These structures are now in ruins, though one may see that they were once very beautiful. Standing in the Forum one can cast his eye over the ruins of the Temple of Vespasian, of Castor and Pollux, of Romulus, and several others; the Arch of Septimius Severus; the Column of Phocus, described by Byron as

"The nameless column with a buried base;"

the Arch of Titus, and several other ruins of great magnificence and renown. Not far distant he sees the Via Sacra, the famous walk of Horace, and the promenade of philosophers and orators, whose names the world has lost. Going out from the Forum to explore the city, the stranger will find ruins of all kinds. The Palace of the Cæsars, the Golden House of Nero, tell us how the sovereigns of ancient Rome used to live. The walls that yet exist, though the decorations are gone; the patches of pavements set in marble or precious stones; the arches, though overgrown with ivy and cypress, and clothed and obstructed with rubbish, tell us that magnificence now unknown once abode in ancient Rome.

The Baths were immense buildings that still remain to tell of imperial luxury. The Baths of Agrippa cover an area of three hundred and fifty thousand square feet, those of Caracalla cover an area of three hundred and twenty thousand square feet, while those of Constantine, Diocletian, and others were still more extensive. These baths show us how extensive and magnificent were the works of this ancient city, and give us an idea of the wealth which was lavished on everything.

The remains of circus and amphitheatre are very numerous. Foremost in the list stands the Coliseum. Erected for gladiatorial shows within fifty years after the death of Christ, it was afterwards used for the slaughter of Christians by wild beasts. The structure is now crumbling to pieces. For eighteen centuries it has stood, one of the chief monuments of Rome. The arena is two hundred and eighty-seven feet long, and one hundred and eighty feet wide; from the arena the seats rise tier on tier, one hundred and fifty feet. The immense size of the building may be gathered from the fact that eighty-seven thousand persons could be seated, while in the arena one hundred men, and a like number of wild beasts, could fight at once, and have sufficient room. In the Middle Ages it was used for a fortress, and the Roman princes have despoiled it of its beauties by taking away its ornaments to decorate their own palaces. The exterior view of the structure presents us with four stories, composed of arches, piers, and columns, with windows and doors. The lower story is of the Doric order; the second of the Ionic order; the third of the Corinthian; the fourth also is Corinthian. Beneath the structure, under the seats, is a vast number of cells, where the beasts who fought in the arena were kept. The building is now used occasionally for religious worship. A huge wooden cross stands in the centre, and any person going up to it and imprinting upon it a kiss, is promised an indulgence of two hundred days. This is a very fortunate arrangement for those poor sinners who believe in the power of men to grant indulgences, and who wish, while on a visit to Rome, to indulge in an unusual number of sins.

The time to visit the Coliseum is by moonlight, when the pale beams come struggling through the broken arches. This was the time when Byron used to go and catch inspiration from the scene, and

ARCH OF SEPTIMIUS SEVERUS.

others who have followed his example have felt the same emotions of awe and grandeur as they have stood at midnight in the arena once wet with blood, now guarded by a peaceful cross, and looked upon the ruined corridors, black frowning pillars, gloomy, cavernous arches, and remembered what scenes had there transpired, since Christian blood was used to cement the mortar in the walls, to this hour, when murder and crime have ceased their empire here, and beggary and scepticism have taken the place of blood and groans.

The Anglo-Saxon pilgrims who gazed upon the Amphitheatre in the Middle Ages, perfect then after ages of change, predicted for it an immortality: —

"While stands the Coliseum, Rome shall stand;
When falls the Coliseum, Rome shall fall;
And when Rome falls, the world."

Who can say this prediction will not prove true, for Rome is reeling, decaying, falling as the Coliseum is crumbling, and who knows that they both may not behold the

"Wreck of matter and the crush of worlds."

The Theatre of Pompey dates back further than the Coliseum, but is not in so good a state of preservation; indeed the Palazzo Pio is built over the ruins, concealing a part of them. The descriptions of this edifice show that it must have been a grand and noble work of art. It was built by Pompey, but the people having charged him with using it to corrupt the morals of Rome, he erected against it a temple to Venus Victrix, and thus set his worship of the gods against the injury he was doing to public morals. Near this theatre stood the Senate-house, where Cæsar fell, smitten by Brutus whom he had befriended, and whose death poets and orators have used to point their eloquence and inspire their address. These amphitheatres are found all through Rome, and their ruins attest their ancient greatness and grandeur. The Theatre of Balbus, though the smallest that still retains its form, would hold eleven thousand five hundred persons. The Theatre of

Marcellus would hold thirty thousand people. In the Circus Maximus nearly two hundred thousand persons could be convened, and were accommodated with seats. The Circus of Romulus presents a ground plan of fifteen hundred and eighty feet in length, and two hundred and sixty feet in breadth, and an immense number of persons could have been accommodated within its walls. Of course the ruins are now, many of them, but little more than heaps of rubbish and stone, but enough remains to mark the spots, and show us what these structures were when the warlike Romans, with their wives and daughters, assembled within their walls.

The columns that remain standing also have histories, and teach useful lessons to every stranger. The Column of Phocus has been referred to. For a long time no one could tell what event it was erected to commemorate, or the deeds of what sage, poet or hero it was designed to perpetuate. You remember that Byron alludes to it thus:

"Tully was not so eloquent as thou,
Thou nameless column with a buried base."

The "buried base" has been relieved of rubbish, and the column has found a name and a history. It is a Corinthian shaft, resting on a substantial pedestal, and was erected in 608.

The Column of Trajan, erected in 114, a mixture of Tuscan, Doric, and Corinthian, covered with bass-reliefs, the top of which is reached by a flight of one hundred and eighty-five steps, is one of the finest of the remains of the past. The ancients were accustomed to record their victories on these monuments; and all over the base of the Trajan Column are beautiful carvings representing several important battles and other historical events. Once the colossal statue of Trajan stood on the top of the tall shaft. In his hand was a golden orb, which contained his ashes after he was dead.

But long since the imperial image passed away, and since then other forms have been placed there, also to disappear. Other columns rise amid these ruins, each with its memorable history. The Column of Duilius, to commemorate his victories over the Carthaginians; of Antoninus Pius, which once, in its rich, quaint massiveness, won the attention of all; that of Marcus Aurelius, with its historical emblems, and now surmounted with a statue of St. Paul, and others of note, some cast down, some standing erect, speak of great Rome, her mighty past, and her sad decline.

The arches, many of which still stand, give evidence of great taste on the part of those who reared them. The Arch of Drusus, on the famous old Appian Way, now overgrown with ivy; the Arch of Septimius Severus, erected by goldsmiths and bankers, to a family of their craft, profusely ornamented and elaborately carved; the Arch of Titus, a grand monument of the conquest of Jerusalem and the complete overthrow of the Jews, bearing inscriptions and covered with bass-reliefs emblematic of scenes in that bloody reign, when God put to the lips of the Jewish nation a cup of blood; the Arch of Constantine, composed of fragments of one more ancient, covered with beautiful carvings and rich designs, a history in itself of an empire's glory and renown. All these are monuments of the former magnificence of this city, which now lies a heap of stones and mounds of earth. As we go groping about amid these ruins, we cross and recross the renowned Appian Way, a broad road which led through the city, the pride of the ancient Romans. The pavement was of marble, or volcanic stones, and was very beautiful. The houses which were erected near it were costly, and some of the most noted tombs are now ranged alongside of it. The ancients were accustomed to build their tombs above the ground, and many of them were afterward used for fortifications. On this Via Appia stands the tomb of Cæcelia Metella. Nineteen hundred years ago, before Christ appeared in Bethlehem, this structure rose, a circular tower nearly one hundred feet high; and to-day, when its history is almost forgotten, and even the people who live at its base do not know its name, or who Cæcelia Metella was, it seems about as perfect as ever. When the memory of the illustrious woman who first reposed in it had passed away, it was used as a fortress, and again and again has withstood the furious assaults of war. The tomb of this renowned woman is immortalized in " Childe Harold ":

> " There is a stern round tower of other days,
> Firm as a fortress, with its fence of stone,
> Such as an army's baffled strength delays,
> Standing with half its battlements alone,
> And with two thousand years of ivy grown,
> The garland of eternity, where wave
> The green leaves over all by time o'erthrown ; —
> What was this tower of strength ? within its cave
> What treasure lay so locked, so hid ? — A woman's grave.
>
> " But who was she, the lady of the dead,
> Tomb'd in a palace ? Was she chaste and fair ?
> Worthy a king's — or more — a Roman's bed ?
> What race of chiefs and heroes did she bear ?
> What daughter of her beauties was the heir ?
> How lived — how loved — how died she ? Was she not
> So honor'd — and conspicuously there,
> Where meaner relics must not dare to rot,
> Placed to commemorate a more than mortal lot ?
>
> " Perchance she died in youth : it may be, bow'd
> With woes far heavier than the ponderous tomb
> That weighed upon her gentle dust, a cloud
> Might gather o'er her beauty, and a gloom
> In her dark eye, prophetic of the doom
> Heaven gives its favorites — early death ; yet shed
> A sunset charm around her, and illume
> With hectic light, the Hesperus of the dead,
> Of her consuming cheek the autumnal leaf-like red.
>
> " Perchance she died in age — surviving all,
> Charms, kindred, children — with the silver-gray
> On her long tresses, which might yet recall,
> It may be, still a something of the day
> When they were braided, and her proud array
> And lovely form were envied, praised, and eyed
> By Rome — but whither would Conjecture stray ?
> Thus much alone we know — Metella died,
> The wealthiest Roman's wife : Behold his love or pride ! "

The tomb of Publius is yet a massive building, and more than eighteen hundred years old, and seems likely to behold the rise and fall of generations more. The tomb of the Baker, one of the most singular of all the sepulchres of Rome, about fifteen hundred years old, and covered with emblems illustrative of the baker's business: rows of stones, representing loaves of bread, bass-reliefs of the different processes of bread-making, effigies of the baker and his wife selling bread, and all the various designs of the bakers' trade. The tomb of Augustus, built before Christ's time, was two hundred and twenty feet in diameter, but is now in ruins, and its former glory can hardly be discovered.

And so all through ancient Rome you find vast piles, erected for the repose of the dead, now converted into fortresses and military arsenals. Even the Fortress of St. Angelo, a castle holding the same relation to Rome that the Tower does to London, and the Bastile once did to Paris, was formerly the tomb of Hadrian. It is an immense building, having provisions for a large garrison, cells for one hundred and fifty prisoners, and the various equipments for the defence of the city.

While among these ruins one naturally inquires for the Tarpeian Rock, so famous in Rome's history. This rock is on the southern side of the Capitoline, and is not so much of a precipice as when the traitors were made to leap from its summit, and dash themselves to pieces on the stones below. The descent is about seventy feet, and it was sure death to him who was forced to leap from it.

Near the Tarpeian Rock is the famous Mamertine prison, where the Apostle Paul was confined previous to his martyrdom. There are two chambers hewn out of the rock, both of them beneath the ground. A flight of twenty-eight steps leads us down into the upper prison, a room about thirty feet by twenty-five. The lower prison is smaller, and is called the Tullian prison. In this cell is a stone pillar to which the Apostle was chained, and here have been perpe-

CASTLE AND BRIDGE OF ST. ANGELO.

trated some of the vilest cruelties against humanity. A little door leads from this prison into the dark catacombs which extend in all directions under the city. I had a curiosity to explore these dark abodes, and taking a torch I went into the passage. My friends, to startle me, threw back the door behind me, and it closed with a dull,

IN THE FORUM LOOKING TOWARD THE CAPITOL.

heavy sound which grated terribly on the nerves. Scarcely had I taken a step forward when my torch, striking against a jutting rock, was extinguished. The feeling of that moment I can hardly describe. There was a sense of loneliness, a dismal foreboding which made the moment I stayed there absolutely awful. The slime and mud was thick and gluey beneath my feet; now and then I could feel the loathsome lizard as he sprang against my person; I scarcely dared to move lest in those winding passages I should be lost, and unable to find the door, and though I was not foolish enough to make any outcry, I was inexpressibly glad when my friends opened the door and let the glare of their torches show me the way back to them.

THE MAMERTINE PRISON.

It was my privilege to explore the catacombs from another point, and to become better acquainted with those regions of darkness. These vaults, which underlie the whole city of Rome, were doubtless excavations made to secure the stone for building purposes; the excavations having been made they were used for burial-grounds, and in niches all along the subterranean passages may be found the ashes of the forgotten dead. When persecution spread its wings over the

Eternal City, the early Christians fled to these retreats, and the persecutors, on account perhaps of the narrowness of the passages, which enabled a few persons to hold out against great numbers, and perhaps on account of superstitious reverence for the dwelling-place of the dead, did not follow them. There those holy people chanted their sacred anthems, and there did they commune with each other and with God. The catacombs have been despoiled of many of their inscriptions and relics, which have been placed in the Vatican, and these subterranean abodes are the haunts of thieves and outcasts. We entered some distance, and were content.

The best preserved monument of ancient Rome is the Pantheon, which, though built before the time of Christ, is in better condition than some stone churches in England and America which have not been erected two hundred years. It has been in turn devoted to idols and to God, to Jove and to Jesus; and now every day here within its walls is heard the chant of the priest and the song of the mourner. But I have spent as much time as I can afford on the ruins of Rome, and yet much more remains to be said. The temples of Bacchus, of Concord, of Juno Matuta, of Minerva, of Mars, and many others, all renowned, yet stand; the gates, the bridges, the pyramid of Caius Cestus, and many other objects of interest, all make a dozen letters necessary to give an idea of what they are; but we must pass over them, and leave this old dead city for one of life and activity.

Looking down from the Capitol, the best view of the new city of Rome, or that part which is still inhabited, is obtained. The Capitol stands on the Capitoline hill, and I remember one day clinging to its tower, and with my arm wound around the colossal image on its summit, looking off upon the city, as it lay before my eyes. The Corso black with human life, the Tiber flowing through the city, the old castle of St. Angelo, with the French flag floating over it, St. Peter's Church, the noblest in the world, were all full in view. St. John Lateran, the mother of churches, lifting up its front, the

Vatican, the Inquisition House, and the various places of interest were taken in at a single glance. Until the conquest of Victor Emanuel, Rome had the worst government in the world. The pope was the supreme head of the civil and religious power; the cardinals, seventy-two in number, constitute a sacred college, and there were minor municipal officers, whose powers all emanate directly or indirectly from the sovereign head. The population of the city is about two hundred and seventy-five thousand persons: of this number ten thousand are Jews, sixteen hundred peasants, two thousand five hundred monks, two thousand nuns, with many other useless characters. The streets are full of beggars of the lowest and most despicable description, and one tires of their ceaseless plea for aid.

Our time is so limited that we shall only be able to skip from place to place in the city, noticing the things which are most peculiar and interesting. And the first object of interest is St. Peter's, a wonderful edifice, the fame of which is as extensive as that of Rome herself. A religious house was built on this spot as early as A. D. 90, but the great edifice was not commenced in earnest until 1506, when Julius II. entered upon it with great vigor, and it was completed in 1590, or eighty-four years after its foundations were laid. But changes were constantly made, and additions built, that lead historians to give the time of building as one hundred and seventy-six years, and still further we find that the building was not completed until three hundred years after its commencement, though the massive edifice was completed in less than one century. The cost of the building one hundred years ago had reached the enormous sum of sixty million dollars, and the mere repairs annually amount to more than thirty thousand dollars. The buildings cover two hundred and forty thousand square feet, and are monstrous in their extent. The workmen who are employed to repair the edifice have cottages on the roof, and live there with their families, and the latter seldom come down into the world below. The exterior of St. Peter's is well known. There are so many pictures of it, that I need give no description. The semicircular colonnades, composed of two hundred and eighty immense columns, enclosing an area which is beautifully ornamented; the façade from plans of Carlo Moderno, concealing the front of the building; the dome towering up towards the clouds, are all so familiar that I waste no time on them. The effect on entering the church is wonderful: you are struck with solemn awe, and yet when asked to say what so overwhelms you, you can hardly tell. You may recollect that Byron, in Childe Harold, in speaking of this church, after saying that

> " Power, glory, strength, and beauty — all are aisled
> In this eternal ark of worship undefiled,"

bids us

> "Enter; its grandeur overwhelms thee not:
> And why? It is not lessened: but the mind,
> Expanded by the genius of the spot,
> Has grown colossal, and can only find
> A fit abode, wherein appear enshrined,
> Thy hopes of immortality."

The immense size of the cathedral does not at once strike the mind; it grows upon us. It measures in length six hundred and eight feet; the height of the nave is one hundred and fifty feet; the length of the transept is four hundred and fifty feet; the height of the dome, from the pavement to the summit, inside, is four hundred and five, and from the pavement to the top of the cross, outside, is four hundred and thirty-five feet. Several churches as large as the average could be dragged about inside, and the steeple of the Trinity Church with Grace Church on top of it, could stand beneath the dome.

The high altar stands directly beneath the dome. This high altar is a most expensive thing, and stands, we are told, directly over the grave of St. Peter. The expense of the altar may be judged from the canopy over it, of solid bronze, the most inexpensive part of the whole, being cast by Bernini from bronze stolen from the noble Pantheon in 1633, which cost one hundred and ten thousand dollars. It

GENERAL VIEW OF ST. PETER'S AND THE VATICAN.

was at this high altar that I saw the pope, the successor of St. Peter. I was there on Corpus Christi day, when in grand procession the pontiff rode upon the shoulders of men. The procession was composed of priests, monks and other church dignitaries, and in the midst of them his Holiness, as the Catholics call him, was seated in a chair, with a canopy over his head, and borne by eight or ten distinguished personages. The chanting multitude passed through the cathedral, down the colonnade, and out into the city. The pope held a cross in his hand, and had all the appearance of being a little seasick.

St. Peter's Church contains many fine statues and paintings, and many elaborate chapels. Here, monarchs, popes, and cardinals have been buried in solemn state, and hours might be spent in the description of their sepulchres.

I ascended the dome, by a stone-paved staircase between the dome and its inside lining. This staircase is so gradual in its ascent that horses have been used to convey up the visitors. On the roof we find the houses of the workmen, the shops in full operation, a fountain of water playing in the sun, and various signs of life and animation. Weary and faint we reach the ball, which is large enough to hold sixteen persons. From that point the view is very fine indeed. Before us is the city, full of life; out beyond are the ruins of old Rome, and still beyond, stretching out in every direction, is the wide, dreary Campagna, limited by the Apennines and the blue Mediterranean. Once a year, during the Holy Week, this cathedral is illuminated, and probably such a display can be found no where else on earth. The illumination takes place three nights in succession. Several hundred men are employed to light the lights, which are hung all over the dome and on the front of the immense building. The first part of the illumination is called the silver illumination, the lights being concealed in screens of white paper. There they hang, making the cathedral look as if it were a vast orb of silver flashing on the night. At nine

THE POPE GIVING THE BENEDICTION ON PALM SUNDAY.

o'clock the golden illumination begins. A thousand broad lamps flash out instantaneously; others follow by hundreds, until the cathedral seems in a perfect blaze. The lamps used for the golden illumination are iron vessels filled with pitch and tar; and about seven thousand of them are used, and they burn until midnight.

From St. Peter's we go to the Church of St. John Lateran. The chapter of this cathedral takes precedence of St. Peter's, and the papal coronations are held here. When a pope dies the cardinals assemble, close the doors, and proceed to the election of his successor. Sometimes several days are spent in vain. The people know the room in which the election takes place, and wait uneasily to know the result. When a choice is made the ballots are all taken and thrown into the grate and set on fire; and the smoke which issues from the chimney is the first intelligence the people have that a pope has been chosen. An official then comes forth to the city and proclaims that the choice has been made, and announces the name of the favored one. The coronation always takes place in St. John Lateran, and is very imposing. Five general councils have been held here, and within these walls decisions have been reached which have shaken the world. In this church is the famous baptistery in which Rienzi bathed on the night before his death. It is believed that in this baptistery Constantine was baptized.

Rome is full of churches and cathedrals, and all of them are famous for some particular things. In most of them are relics, the bones of saints, and other senseless things. The church of S. Maria della Concezione (church of the Capucines), has in the vaults beneath a quantity of holy soil, brought from Jerusalem. When the monks die, they are buried here awhile, and then their bones are taken up, scraped, prepared, and clothed with their former habits, and thus they remain awhile, when they are taken to pieces and the bones piled together, skulls in one place, and other bones elsewhere. Figures, formed of bones, are on the walls. Crosses of bones are on the ceil-

ON THE CAMPAGNA.

ings. A few skeletons are standing around uncovered, and the whole place is abhorrent to the feelings and disgusting to the senses.

In one church you will find pieces of the true cross, in another the napkin with which the blood was wiped from the fainting brow of Christ as he went to the cross. One of the most noted relics at Rome is the Scala Santa, or Holy Staircase. The story runs that this staircase was the identical one over which Christ went into the judgment hall of Pontius Pilate. There are twenty-eight steps of marble, and no one is allowed to ascend them except on his knees. The complete conversion of Martin Luther took place when he was ascending on his knees these stairs. The consciousness of the folly of the whole scene came upon him, and he arose and strode away repeating, "The just shall live by faith." About half-way up these stairs is a spot on the marble that looks like blood, and the monks say that this stain is the blood of Jesus, he having paused as he went out of the hall, and cast back a reproachful look at the cowardly governor who had condemned him. These may be the stones of that judgment hall. The thing is in no wise impossible, and many persons who repudiate the superstitions of the papal church believe this statement.

Near the Cathedral of St. Peter stands the Vatican, the palace of the pope. This building existed one thousand years ago, and has received additions and improvements until it is a vast, irregular, unsightly structure; but forming one of the most gorgeous palaces in the world. It is eleven hundred and fifty-one feet long, and seven hundred and sixty-eight feet broad. It has eight grand staircases, and two hundred of less dimensions; twenty-two courts admit air and light; and four thousand four hundred and twenty apartments compose the interior of the building. What it cost no one can tell, and its present value scarcely any one could estimate. Within the palace is the famous Sistine chapel, where mass is said by the pope, and where the papal throne stands. It is in this chapel that the visitor sees the grandest fresco in the world—the Last Judgment, of Michel Angelo, sixty feet by thirty, grand in its conception, noble in its design, and faultless in its execution. The joy of the righteous, the sorrow of the lost, the groups of figures, the awful throne, the Great Judge, are all admirably represented, and awe impresses one as he gazes on this sublime work of art.

But you know that the Vatican is famous not merely as the abode of the pope, and the place where priestly conclaves are held, but as a vast receptacle of works of genius. The collections of paintings, the galleries of sculpture, the halls of art, are the finest in the world. In this short letter I hardly dare say anything about them. They are so vast and indescribable that no justice could be done them, nor could I give you an intelligible idea of them. There is Raphael's Transfiguration, which was hung over his corpse, to be worshipped as a thing divine. Multitudes come to see it, and,

> "Entering in, they looked,
> Now on the dead, then on that masterpiece;
> Now on his face, lifeless and colorless,
> Then on those forms divine, that lived and breathed,
> And would live on for ages."

Here too is Domenichino's Communion of St. Jerome, and many others of the noblest taste, and executed in the highest style of art.

The galleries of sculpture are as rich as the collections of paintings. The cabinets of coin, medals, and all the vast variety of things, peculiar to such a collection, are of great value. Here is the Laocoön, a specimen of sculpture called by Michel Angelo "the wonder of art," and which Pliny declared to be "a work superior to all others, both in painting and statuary." The position of the giant Laocoön and his children, in the folds of the serpent, the despair and anguish depicted on the face of the father, and the touching expressions of the children, have been so often described in sober prose, melodious poetry, and striking paintings and drawings, that no effort of description is needed. The piece of statuary forms, perhaps, the most renowned expression of

"A father's love, and mortal agony,
With an immortal patience blending."

We also find here the Apollo Belvedere, another of the finest specimens of ancient sculpture, which the artists of our time in vain endeavor to imitate. Here, too, we find the Genius of the Vatican, and the Sleeping Cleopatra, which have been made immortal by the finest of the poet's lays. Days, weeks, years may be spent in these vast halls, amid Egyptian wonders and Persian splendors, conversing with the masters of the fine arts, with Michel Angelo, Praxiteles, Raphael, Sacchini, Titian, and a host of others.

But the wonder of the building to me was the library, the richest collection of books and manuscripts in the world, different popes having added to it since its foundation in the fourteenth century. The printed books, not large in number, only fifty thousand, do not form the richest or most valuable part of the collection, though these alone, from the rareness of the works, would make the collection the most valuable on earth. The library derives its value from its six hundred Hebrew, seven hundred and fifty Arabic, and four hundred and sixty Syriac manuscripts, and from a vast number of others in the Coptic, Ethiopic, Turkish, Persian, Sarmatian, Sclavonic, Armenian, and Chinese. There is here a Bible of the sixth century, and other manuscripts going back to the third and fourth centuries. The value of some of these manuscripts is very great, and many of them have no duplicates in the world.

There are many other public and private palaces in Rome, all of which are, to a greater or less extent, open to the public, and which are filled with works of art, libraries, and other valuable things. All of these are noted in the history of the Eternal City, and some of them have been baptized in blood.

Near St. Peter's Church stands the Palace of the Inquisition, used yet as a religious prison for monks who have been accused of heresy, and priests who have abandoned their faith. What dark deeds transpired in this house of woe none can tell, and probably it will be long ere its blood-stained passages will reveal their mysteries.

The Capitol I have already referred to. It is a grand structure, on the Capitoline Hill, and is the State House of Rome. Besides being a public edifice for the transaction of business, it has extensive galleries of art, which in some respects rival those of the Vatican. Here is the famous nursing wolf,

> "The thunder-stricken nurse of Rome,
> Scorched by the Roman Jove's ethereal dart,"

emblem of the humble agent that nurtured the life of Romulus. She has in turn been celebrated by Dionysius, Livy, Cicero, and Byron, as the

> "Mother of the mighty heart."

And here, too, we find the Dying Gladiator, which has been admired by critics from Pliny to John Bell, the latter of whom describes the statue as "all nature, all feeling," which has been immortalized in song and poetry for hundreds of years.

Among the objects of interest to a stranger in Rome, is the English burial-ground, near the pyramid of Caius Cestus, just by the Porta San Paolo. Everywhere else in Rome the traveller sees strange names, but when he reaches this spot he sees familiar names and epitaphs written in his own language. Everything is quiet, and the place seems like a little sanctuary saved from the pollutions and superstitions of that great city. Here lies Percy Bysshe Shelley, the freethinker, who made his own life and that of his friends wretched, and who, persisting in his atheism until death, as if to do all he could to defeat a resurrection, ordered his body burnt, and his ashes scattered. Lord Byron and Leigh Hunt did the work, and the poor flesh was consumed, leaving the heart unburnt. The heart and ashes were entombed here, and the "Cor Cordium"—heart of hearts—attracts the gaze of the stranger as he approaches the spot. That is true which they wrote on the tomb as to his earthly works,—true of his fate, though he denied it while alive:—

> "Nothing of him that doth fade,
> But doth suffer a sea change
> Into something rich and strange."

Shelley was first wrecked, then burnt, then buried, but God can find his dust.

Richard Wyatt is buried in these grounds. John Bell slumbers here. John Keats, who anticipated literary fame and pure happiness in the walks of a virtuous literature, and who died broken-hearted, rests here beneath the soil, and on his tomb is this inscription: "This grave contains all that was mortal of a young English poet, who, on his death-bed, in the bitterness of his heart at the malicious power of his enemies, desired these words to be engraven on his tombstone,— 'Here lies one whose name is writ in water.'"

This graveyard is filled up with those who have gone on excursions of pleasure, or on pilgrimages of piety, or to recover failing health, or to search for genius amidst the classic scenes of Italy, but who, instead of finding pleasure, health, or fame, have laid their bones to rest beneath the soil of a strange land.

The impressions of a stranger in Rome are most sad and sorrowful. If he comes here in the summer, he will see a desolate city, the buildings dull and dingy, the streets filled with filthy beggars, and the pall of death hanging over everything. Nothing but a few religious observances, such as that of Corpus Christi day, will relieve the monotony of the scene, and as he floats down the Tiber, goes into St. Angelo, or St. Peter's, or walks languidly along the Corso, he will feel that he is in a city under a curse. The very breath he draws seems to come hard from his laboring lungs, and though everything he sees is invested with interest, yet he leaves Rome with a sort of feeling that

CASTLE OF SAN ELMO.

one experiences when, after he has walked through the wards of a prison, and seen the handcuffs, the cells, the closed windows, he goes out and stands in the free air, and beneath the clear sunlight.

If one goes to Rome in the winter, he finds a city occupied by crowds of strangers, and strangely blending religious observances with the most depraved and senseless dissipation. The religious observances are very funny specimens of religion, such as washing pilgrims' feet, a dozen men riding the pope on their shoulders, candles, and crosses, and penances, all mingled up in one confused mass.

The feet-washing scene occurs in Holy Week, and the cardinals wash the feet of the pilgrims who come here to worship. These pilgrims sit in rows, each with a bowl of water under his feet. And the cardinals and other high officials who are accustomed to ride in carriages, and dwell in state, who at any other time would kick the very same lazy beggars from their path without ceremony, are seen passing from one to another, scrubbing the dirt which had been collecting a year, from the feet which are thrust into the bowls. J. T. Headley, when he saw this operation, says that there were several dirty, filthy Roman boys who had come in to get washed, and one of them attracted his attention. He was half frightened and half roguish, and between the curious gaze of the spectators, the odd position he was in, and the cardinal in his awful robes at his feet, his countenance had a half-scared and half-comic look, and his eye rolled from the cardinal to the spectators, and back again, in queer bewilderment. This senseless and disgusting performance can hardly be pleasant to those who do the washing, however gratifying it may be to those whose feet are washed. If I was going to do the washing, I should wish to do it with a brush, on the end of a ten-foot pole.

The Carnival in Rome is always celebrated with a great deal of foolish merriment and nonsense. The city during the period resembles almost anything else than a religious place. The ceremonies consist of masquerades, balls, theatricals, midnight revels, and all sorts of dissipation. On the few last days of the Carnival, the people all turn out, and with masks and in various disguises are found in the street. All kinds of dress are put on, all kinds of hats are worn, and all turn to pelting each other with confectionery, paper-flowers and other such harmless missiles. People at the windows pelt those in the streets; those in the carriages pelt those in the windows, and every madcap fancy is carried out. When night comes the scene changes. All these thousands of people are provided with curious-colored, fantastic torches and lanterns, and the game consists in each one keeping his own light burning, and extinguishing that of his neighbor. Noblemen and beggars engage in the rush. Royal ladies, queenly dames, unbend, and in the wild rush of the crowd are as eager to cut up some new prank as are little children. A horse-race closes up the whole. It is not such a horse-race as we have at home and in England, but the horses are painted, and let loose in the Corso, and without riders, go dashing onward, plunging through a paper screen stretched across one end of the street.

The Roman Catholic religion is seen at Rome in all its greatness and splendor. We only have side views of it in our country. Here is its seat and centre. The gorgeous carriages of the cardinals are seen dashing through the streets; the monks, Benedictines, Franciscans, Dominicans, white, black and gray friars are seen all over the city. And a set of ignoble-looking creatures they are. They have on a coarse habit, which flaps about their naked legs, as if it was inhabited by a skeleton, their heads are always bare, and are shaved in various ways, and they move about with beads and crosses hung to the leathern girdle which they wear. Some of them are men of much learning, having little else to do than study. But dressed and shaven as they are, they all look like idiots or knaves. Convents and religious houses are all over the city, in which the nuns and monks dwell, practising the rites of the church to which they belong.

All around, the people give evidence of the rule under which they are. The wealthy people of Rome are generally very wealthy. They are composed very largely of extensive landholders in the vicinity, who build rich residences in the city, and draw their revenues from the country round about. Some of these landholders own two hundred thousand acres each of rich land, highly productive, and under a high state of cultivation. This is all let out in small farms, at enormous rents. There is scarcely any middle-class between these wealthy landholders and the humble and half-starved poor. The former class are treading on the necks of the latter. There is no city in the world where so many people live without work as in Rome. The monks do not work; the landholders do not work; the city officials do not work; the beggars do not work; the Jews do not work; and we were puzzled to find anybody that did. The climate is conducive to indolent habits, and the very breezes that fan your temples seem to be lazy and indolent in their movements.

The churches of Rome are very rich in their construction and adornments, and should a small part of the money expended on them be given to the poor, or laid out in public improvements, we should soon see a mighty change in Rome. One mean little newspaper, the contents of which are a few columns of papal news, bulls, and advertisements, is all we have seen here in the line of literature. No improvements appear in the city; no signs of public spirit are seen in any direction. But the churches are gorgeous, and barefooted men and bonnetless women sit under arches and lean against pillars which have cost thousands of dollars to rear them. To show the needless expenditure, I may notice a few facts in relation to some of these churches. There prevails an idea that in 251 the body of St. Paul was removed from the Vatican and buried out on the Campagna, some one or two miles out on the road to Ostia. So this church, which has its millions of paupers, erected a church over the spot. So dreadful was the malaria that no habitation could be seen near the place, and in certain seasons the spot could be visited only at the risk of life. But the church went up; not a neat, small monumental pile; but a huge edifice, four hundred and eleven feet long, the roof of which was supported by one hundred and thirty-eight beautiful marble columns, and all the details of which were carried out in almost unequalled splendor. This structure was destroyed by fire, so that the walls were rendered useless and were taken down, and Rome, which keeps the epistles of Paul from the dying people, at once set herself to build a new church, of still greater beauty, over the Apostle's grave. In 1825 (more than a half of a century ago) the new church was commenced, and it is yet hardly finished, and millions of dollars have already been spent upon it. Beautiful columns of Egyptian alabaster, sixty feet high, and procured at a fabulous expense, stand in their places. The portraits of two hundred and fifty-eight popes, beginning with Peter and running down to Pio Nono, not on poor canvas, but in rich stone mosaic, prepared from coins and medals, decorate a portion of the walls; and one is amazed at the vastness and grandeur of the plans. For such mammoth expenditures the people are taxed, and hard earnings are wrung from the honest poor to erect these useless and extravagant temples of pride.

There is scarcely one of the churches of Rome which is not famous for something curious. The people go to a particular church to worship, not because it is convenient, but because the church is famed for something, and there are very few of them which do not have some tradition to make them sacred, or some relics, a sight of which is supposed to confer peculiar indulgences on the worshipper. In St. Peter's Cathedral there are kept records of these things: a column, which the traveller is told was the one against which Christ leaned in the temple when he disputed with the doctors, and which is said to have been brought from Jerusalem; the handkerchief with which Christ wiped his face when he was on the way to the cross, the form of the face marked in blood still being seen; a piece of the true cross. Some years ago the latter was stolen, probably for the jewels which had been set in it. For a long time it was missing, large rewards were offered for it, a great ado was made about it. It was found, just outside the city, with the jewels broken out. All Rome had a jubilee when it was discovered. It was placed in a glass coffer, laid on a car, and a great procession drew it back to its old place in St. Peter's. Of course profane people are never allowed to see these relics. None but leaders of the Church ever look upon them.

The Church of Santa Croce also has a piece of the true cross, and it is shown to the people once a year, in Easter week. Some of the bones of Thomas à Becket are also kept here. The Church of Ara Cæli is famed for the Santissimo Bambino, or wooden baby, a wonderful figure of the Saviour, which the Catholics tell us has miraculous power to cure all kinds of diseases. It was carved by a Franciscan monk, out of wood which grew on the Mount of Olives, and was painted by St. Luke, when the tired monk went to sleep one day.

The Feast of the Baby once a year calls together all the sick people in the region, and wonderful are the cures said to be performed. It was in this church that Gibbon first conceived the idea of writing the "Decline and Fall of the Roman Empire." All the churches are distinguished for something of interest to those who hold the papal faith. In St. Peter's there is an old bronze statue of Jupiter; it was dug out of the ancient ruins and brought to this church, and here christened as St. Peter. The great toe of one foot is nearly gone, having been kissed away by the millions of pilgrims who have supposed it to be an image of the apostle, and have worshipped it as such.

And now we leave Eternal Rome. I wish you could see us getting ready to start, in the lumbering diligence, which has so often been described by travellers, who have made fun of it and scolded about it, but nevertheless have found it a very excellent vehicle in which to be transported from one Italian city to another.

GETTING READY FOR A START.

The objects of interest in Florence are the cathedral, the Baptistery, similar to that of Pisa, and the bell tower; the Pitti Palace, with its museums and galleries of art; the Boboli Gardens, with their rich foliage and shady walks; the convents and churches, rich with works of art; and a large number of public and private edifices, which wealth has adorned and beautified. The cathedral is an odd-looking structure, with a fine dome, from which Michel Angelo modelled that of St. Peter's, in Rome. The dome was the work of Brunelleschi, and is a wonder, which will make his name noted as long as it continues to stand. It is built in alternate layers of black and white stone, and presents a unique appearance.

The Pitti Palace is a very fine structure. It was built by Luca Pitti, who, by a series of misfortunes, became involved in ruin and disgrace. The galleries are filled with the finest paintings, in which are treasured up the works of the old masters. Miles on miles of paintings, and seas on seas of fine carving and chisel-work, are to be found. Here are the evidences of the genius of Titian, Raphael, Rubens, Bartolommeo, Michel Angelo, and a host of the old masters who have now fallen asleep.

On our way to Florence we visited Pisa, where is the wonderful leaning tower, which has seven bells, and is two hundred and seventy-eight feet high. We ascend by a winding staircase, and from the top enjoy a fine prospect of the surrounding country. The deviation is from fifteen to eighteen feet; and as I stood looking down, the danger of falling appeared so great, that I was glad to descend as soon as possible. One naturally clings to the rail of the gallery as he looks down from the dizzy elevation upon the earth beneath, which seems to be passing from under him. Whether the tower was built as it is, in a leaning position, or whether the foundations have settled, is a matter of question, nor can an examination settle the point. I incline to the latter opinion, which accords with the view taken by most travellers.

FLORENCE, FROM THE TERRACE OF SAN MINIATO.

THE BAPTISTERY, PISA.

This group of buildings, with the Campo Santo, forms one of the most interesting objects of study and interest that can be found in Italy. The leaning tower is in itself a wonder, and the whole group, where millions of dollars have been expended, deserves a visit from every person who goes within a hundred miles of the spot.

The Baptistery is an elegant building, standing near the cathedral, giving evidence of the purpose for which it was erected, and the use to which it was put.

VENICE.

Venice was built long ago over the marshes of the Rialto. From an obscure beginning has arisen a great and magnificent city, the centre of a wonderful history, and the home of every practised art and every exalted science. It is built upon seventy-two little islands, connected by three hundred and six bridges, scarcely any of which will admit of any kind of horse-carriage. We anchored in front of the city, and no sooner were we ready to disembark, than we were surrounded with gondolas, propelled rapidly by rowers, all of whom wished to take us to the shore. Throughout the city, where we should have hacks and carriages, they have these gondolas. The gondola is a boat about twenty feet long, very sharp and narrow, and one or two men are generally seen spinning it along the canals or across the harbor. One man can row it as well as two, with one oar as well as two. They have a way of using the oar that they can row very finely on one side. In the centre of the boat is a little pavilion, and beneath this pavilion, to which there are curtains, the voyager sits, as in the body of a coach. We took one of these water-cabs, and were soon landed near the famous Square of St. Mark, crossing which we found ourselves at a comfortable hotel. In Amsterdam and Rotterdam there are about as many streets as canals; but here, properly speaking, there are no streets; for though there are passages, long and narrow, and one can go through the city on foot, yet he sees no carriages, and hears no rumbling of wheels. Every house faces on a canal, and every family has its boat. The city resembles what New York would be if all the streets should sink, and water should fill their places; the public squares surrounded with water; the churches and houses, and all the public buildings facing on streets of water, approached only in boats, or by mean, narrow passages; the water flowing along **Broad-**

way, and whirling around into Park Row, flowing up and down the avenues and lanes, and the people all going shopping in boats, Christian people going to church in boats; men of business going to their places of merchandise in boats. The famous Rialto, or main canal, runs through the city in the form of an inverted S, and that is the Broadway of the city, while out in all directions lead the canals of various sizes. These canals all empty into the Adriatic, which is so near that they are always kept pure.

The Square of St. Mark is on one side of the city, and is an open area of land, built on piles, and is surrounded on all sides by fine buildings, stores, &c., to all of which there are beautiful arcades, and the stores are full of all kinds of showy and ornamental articles. On St. Mark's Square is the famous Cathedral, unlike all others I have ever seen. The Venetians call it the finest church in the world. It combines the Gothic and Oriental styles of architecture, the latter predominating, and the whole building, with its turrets and pinnacles, very much resembles a Mohammedan mosque. As we crossed the threshold we were pointed to the spot on the pavement where the Emperor Frederick Barbarossa and Pope Alexander III. were reconciled, the pope putting his foot upon the neck of the prostrate monarch, and making a formal declaration of his superiority to kings.

Having viewed the Cathedral, which is a curious affair, we went into the Doge's palace, where pride and power once oppressed their subjects, and from which power if not pride has gone out forever. Few buildings in the world have seen more wickedness and witnessed more scenes of degradation than this same palace. The prison, of which all have read, is near the palace, separated from it by a narrow canal, and connected with it by a bridge — the famous Bridge of Sighs. In the days of Venetian pride and glory, no person was ever carried across who returned again to tell what he saw. The bridge leading from the palace to the prison is a mere covered passage, wide enough for three persons to walk abreast. The walls are

GONDOLA.

very thick, and two small windows which admit the light are heavily barred. Thousands have crossed that bridge never to retrace their steps. We saw in the prison three classes of cells: one for the suspected, one for the convicted, and one for the condemned. We also entered chambers where the victims were killed. The instruments of torture that still remain tell of the barbarity of the days gone by. A bare visit to these prisons makes the blood run cold.

Not far distant is the Campanile, or bell-tower. It is a structure forty-two feet square, and three hundred and twenty-three feet high. We ascend inside by an inclined plane, winding round and round, until we reach the top, from which a view of the whole city is obtained. These bell-towers are very common in Europe. Instead of putting the chime of bells on the church, a high tower is built at a little distance, and from its top the sweet tones are emitted.

In our gondola we went from church to church, looking at the pictures and the statuary, and the rich adornments, which give evidence of the taste of a former day. It was amusing to sail along the canals, meeting at every few yards some gondola, occupied now by the man of business returning to his home; now by the man of pleasure seeking recreation; now by the lady of some mansion who has been out to visit a friend, and now by a gay company of very young people who are enjoying themselves as we would on an evening ride. We did not see a mule, horse, donkey, or any such animal during our stay. Indeed, there is scarcely any use for such creatures. All the transportation of the city, the travelling, and the frolicking, is done by water.

The bridges are so made that a carriage cannot cross them. They rise from the side of the canal by steps, and arch over the water beneath. There are numerous questions which arise in the mind of a stranger here, but they are all soon answered. How do the people get along without cellars? Where do the children play? How do the men get to their daily work? And how do the ladies manage to

CATHEDRAL OF ST. MARK

ON THE GRAND CANAL.

show their latest fashions? When we left the city, we were told that the omnibus would start at a certain hour. We repaired to the spot, and found the omnibus to be a boat with a seat running along each side, with rowers, and a conductor. We went through the principal streets, paid our fare, and were landed in season at the dépôt.

Few cities have figured more prominently in the world's history than Venice, and few have more blood upon its record. All about the place are evidences of the barbarism of the past. Over the whole is now an air of decayed splendor, and to all one sees there is a mournful interest. It has long been the home of artists and poets, and some of the finest verses ever written have been inspired by these scenes.

VERONA.

We left Venice late one evening for Verona, and arrived in that city after midnight. We entered an omnibus at the dépôt, scarcely knowing where we were going. Not a soul could speak English, and we could not speak Italian. On we rode; one passenger after another was left at his dwelling, and still on we rode, over a long bridge, through a dark street, beneath the heavy shadow of huge buildings, and at length we reached the hotel. A sleepy porter came out to let us in, and we were at length housed for the rest of the night.

The city of Verona is a very old one, and the traveller finds some few objects of interest which repay his toil and time. Here is seen an ancient amphitheatre in a tolerable state of preservation. It consists of a huge oval structure, without a roof, with seats for perhaps twelve thousand persons. The structure is as perfect and gives as good an idea of such antiquities as does the Coliseum at Rome. The whole is composed of stone, and rests on enormous arches, in which now several miserable families make their abode, where once the wild beasts were kept for the gladiatorial shows.

The tomb of Juliet is here, and for a slight fee is shown to the traveller who wishes to see it. In an old chapel, a stone coffin is found which curious visitors are asked to believe is the tomb of the fictitious character which figures on the pages of Shakespeare. The woman who exhibits it can answer no questions, and the coffin itself does not pay for the time it takes to go and see it.

Getting through with Verona, and paying a visit to Milan, where is the most beautiful cathedral of its architectural order in the world, we one day found ourselves seated in a diligence, which was to take us over the Alps into Switzerland.

RIP VAN WINKLE.

FISHING BY TORCHLIGHT ON THE SWISS LAKES.

IN SWITZERLAND.

CHÂLETS NEAR SEPEY.

ONE evening the Triangle were alone in their meeting. The night was not given up to visitors, and before business was taken up, a miscellaneous talk was indulged in by the boys, who felt an increasing interest in the travels of their Master.

Hal was wild with a project he had formed, and which this evening he proposed to explain to his friends.

"I have an idea which I think will interest you," he said.

"What is it?" asked Will.

"Yes, out with it, old fellow," added Charlie, "an idea is just the thing we want to get hold of."

"Well, it is a good idea."

"Certainly, if you have it, but tell us what it is."

"Why, nothing more than this, that we get the consent of our parents, and go to Europe, and meet Rip Van Winkle and go with him through the rest of his tour."

"Where is the money coming from?"

"Of course our fathers must supply that."

"But will they do it?"

"We can but try them."

This notion was talked over, and the "Triangle" resolved itself into a committee of the whole, to consider the matter and report at some future time. The communication of the Master was then opened.

GENEVA.

One fine afternoon we found ourselves on board the diligence, well seated and on our way for the Alps. From two o'clock till eight we rode through a country of surpassing loveliness. We seemed to be in the midst of a garden all the way along. On we went by Lago Maggiore, and Isola Bella, the seat of Count Borromeo, now by the foot of mountains, and now along by beautiful waters until we arrived at Duomo D'Ossola, a mean Italian town at the foot of the Alps. Headley calls this place "a dirty town, with a smell of garlic," and its "red-capped, mahogany-legged, lazy Lazzaroni, wandering about in it." Here we took supper, getting a beef-steak, half done, and a cup of coffee, half grounds, and at nine o'clock commenced the ascent of the Simplon. We left the beautiful Italian country beneath us and went winding up the Alps; on our ears fell the sound of rushing waters, and above us waved the mountain trees. Up, up, higher we went until we reached the Gorge of Gondo, which is a gallery five hundred and ninety-six feet long, cut out of a rock on the edge of a tremendous precipice. Over this gully the waters roar, and dash, and tumble in mighty torrents. Beautiful cascades go hurrying by the windows of the gallery, and show you how terrible the passage is. All that night we rode on, up higher, the air becoming piercing cold, the roar of the torrents, as they came leaping down from the mountains, more terrible, until at sunrise we reached the highest point, and stood beneath the wooden cross, while spread all around us, on that July day, were fields of ice and snow. Just over the top we found a mean inn, where we took a hearty breakfast, six thousand feet above the sea. Near this inn is a convent, where are several monks, who have dogs of the San Bernard breed, to rescue travellers who may be overtaken by a storm, or who may be so unfortunate as to be within reach of an avalanche. The Simplon pass is at a height of six thousand seven hundred feet; the St. Gothard is six thousand eight hundred feet; the Splugen six thousand eight hundred feet; the Great Bernard eight thousand feet.

These mammoth roads were built by the mighty Napoleon, to carry out his terrible schemes, and the passages which he made over them in the winter must have been tremendous. Every reader of history will remember the terrible Pass of Macdonald over the Splugen, through a mass of avalanches. The passage was made late in November, after frequent snow-storms had filled up the whole roadway. But the hero was not to be deterred by dangers that threatened. Fifteen miles was to be marched in terrible peril. Breast-deep in snow Macdonald led up his soldiers. Now and then the avalanche, thundering with its awful power, came down with its white wings, sweeping away a whole file of men and their mules into the abyss below, leaving a chasm in the serried ranks. Still on they went, leaving the frozen dead all along the track, over whose corpses the wild winds howled a mournful requiem. No one can imagine the terrors of that passage; the avalanche making wide gaps, and hurling the doomed soldiers to certain destruction. From November 26 to December 6, it took that army to cross, and when on the plains of Italy fifteen thousand men stood in battle array, they well might consider it the noblest exploit of modern times.

It took us about five hours to ride down the Simplon on the rocky

BRIEG, ON THE SIMPLON.

ridge, winding back and forth, at times rolling along on the very edge of the tremendous precipice. The first town is Brieg, where we take our morning meal at eleven o'clock. It was a relief to get safely down. Though in summer there is no danger of avalanches, yet the scenery is so wild, and the precipices so numerous, that a sense of relief is felt when one is safe on the plains below. The shape of the mountain gives direction to the avalanche, and certain heavy sounds, heard some time before the mass begins to move, give warning of the danger; yet with all the care which is taken, lives are lost every year, and sometimes carriages are precipitated into the yawning gulfs below. One traveller tells us that a few days before he crossed, the diligence

RAILWAY UP THE RIGI.

was broken into fragments by one of these descending masses of snow. As it was struggling through the deep drifts right in front of one of those gorges where avalanches fall, the driver heard this low, ringing

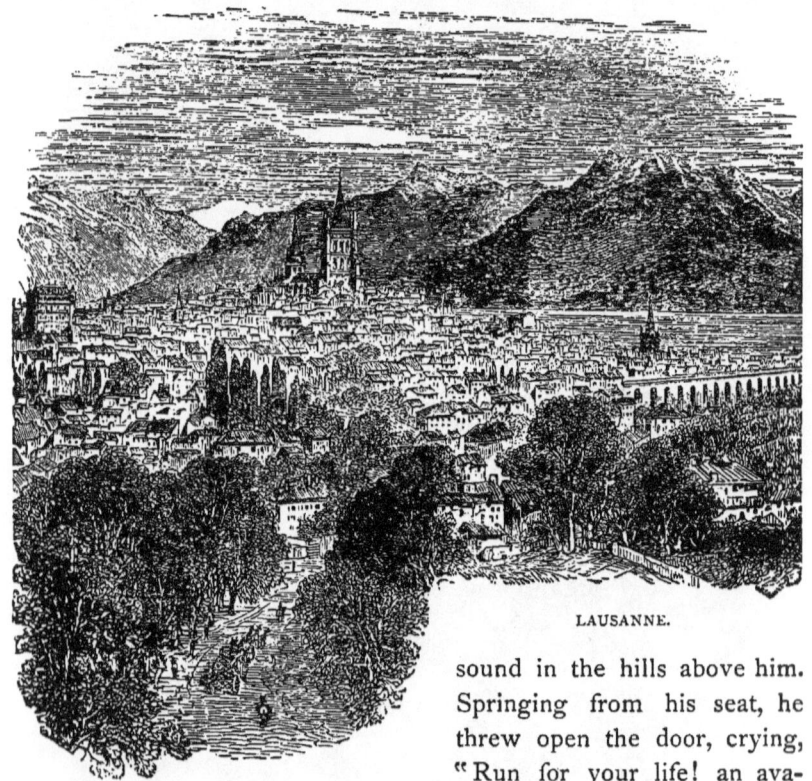

LAUSANNE.

sound in the hills above him. Springing from his seat, he threw open the door, crying, "Run for your life! an avalanche! an avalanche!" and drawing his knife he severed the traces of the horses, and striking them a blow with his whip, sprang ahead. All this was the work of a single minute; the next minute the diligence was in fragments, crushed and buried by the headlong mass.

After escaping from Brieg, we rode through a most charming country, the old mountains towering above us on both sides, while the route along which we travel is decorated with flowers, and fertile as a paradise. At Martigny we stopped all night. This is a place where travellers usually take mules and go to Chamouni, from which place they explore the regions of everlasting ice.

After a hard and very fatiguing ride, we arrived early the next morning at Lausanne, where we tarried awhile. The contrast between this place and the cities on the other side of the Alps was very favorable to the former. We could see that we had passed from a region of filth and indolence to a quiet, industrious, well-ordered country; and Protestant Switzerland, though denied the natural advantages of Papal Italy, seemed to us a paradise compared with the lazy monks and dirty streets of the cities of the pope. Near the hotel at which we took breakfast is the old house of Edward Gibbon, and the garden of our hotel was once the arbor in which he wrote the last page of his work, "The Decline and Fall of the Roman Empire." We wandered over the town, saw whatever was to be seen, and again entering the diligence, started for Geneva.

The towering mountains, covered with perpetual snow, were everywhere and constantly in view. I should fail if I should try to tell you of the pleasure derived in the weeks which succeeded our arrival in the country, in climbing among the pinnacles of crystal, and roaming over the fields of snow. Did space allow, I should write you about the adventures of our little party on the Mer de Glace, our exploits in the valley of Chamouni, the delightful experiences of the Rigi, with visits to shops, towns and villages, all of which you would be glad to hear about. But climbing about among these ice-hills and plains is not child's play. It is hard work and attended with great danger, and sometimes with very laughable adventures.

The ride to Geneva winds along the shores of Lake Leman, and at every turn brings some new scene of beauty to the view. The lake itself, as one says, "lies in the shape of a half-moon, with the horns curved towards the south, and is the largest lake in Switzerland, being fifty-five miles long." The waters are clear, and reflect, as in a polished mirror, the sky, the birds which hover over or fly across it, and the tiny ships which float upon its surface. The banks rise gradually,

ON THE MER DE GLACE.

covered with objects of beauty, from the water-side to the towering mountain, and the eye rests upon a scene of delightful magnificence, wander which way it may, from the lone rock in the sparkling deep,

WRZNAU STATION ON THE RIGI, 1464 FEET ABOVE THE LEVEL OF THE SEA.

on which stands the Castle of Chillon, the prison of Bonnivard, up to the old snow-crowned summit of Mont Blanc.

We arrived at Geneva at nightfall, and after finding a hotel, we

VALLEY OF CHAMOUNI.

walked out to see the out-of-door life of the people. The streets were full of people, and the lighted lamps and shouting voices of the gay ones gave us a very pleasant idea of Geneva. There lived and

TRYING A GLISSADE.

wrote John Calvin, whose power for good has been extended, and whose comments on the Scripture have formed the theological opinions of thousands. We spent our time in looking into the church where Calvin used to preach; in a visit to a new Catholic church about being erected; to the English church where we saw a wedding service; to the old library of Geneva; to the graveyard where Calvin's bones lie without a monument to mark the spot, he having requested that no expensive tomb be built for him. The grave has over it a common piece of granite, on the top of which are the letters "J. C." Beza, when he looked upon this unhonored grave, of one of the greatest of men, took up his pen and wrote:—

Romae ruentis terror ille maximus,
Quem mortuum lugent boni, horrescunt mali,
Ipsa a quo potuit virtutem discere virtus,
Cur adeo exiguo ignotoque in cespite clausus
Calvinus lateat, rogas?
Calvinum assidue comitata modestia vivum
Hoc tumulo manibus condidit ipsa suis,
O te beatum cespitem tanto hospite!
O cui invidere cuncta possint marmora!

CALVIN — of falling Rome the dread,
Whom all the good lament as dead,
While wicked men still fear him, stern,
Virtue from whom might virtue learn —
Sleeps in this *humble* grave. And why?
The voice of truth gives this reply —
'Twas Modesty, his living friend,
Placed this memorial of his end.
O happy grave, with whom is such a guest,
That proudest marbles envy thee, thus blest!

Not only did we go to the grave of the reformer, but also to the house in which Calvin lived, situated in an obscure street. We entered the dark and dismal gateway, and knocked at the door of the room which was once the study of the reformer. Up these very stairs, and into this cheerless study, the men who were associated with Calvin went, and held communion. Kindred spirits they were engaged in a kindred cause. Here those volumes were written which have left such an indelible impress upon the world — indelible because they only echo the teachings of God. Here the prayers were offered which went up to God, and moved his gracious will, and drew upon the supplicant such a measure of the Holy Ghost. Here were arranged those mighty schemes to disenthral the human mind, the influence of which we have not yet, and never shall cease to feel. The house is now occupied by those who scarcely know the name of Calvin, and who look upon those who come with reverence to survey the premises very much as the barbarians of Italy look upon the

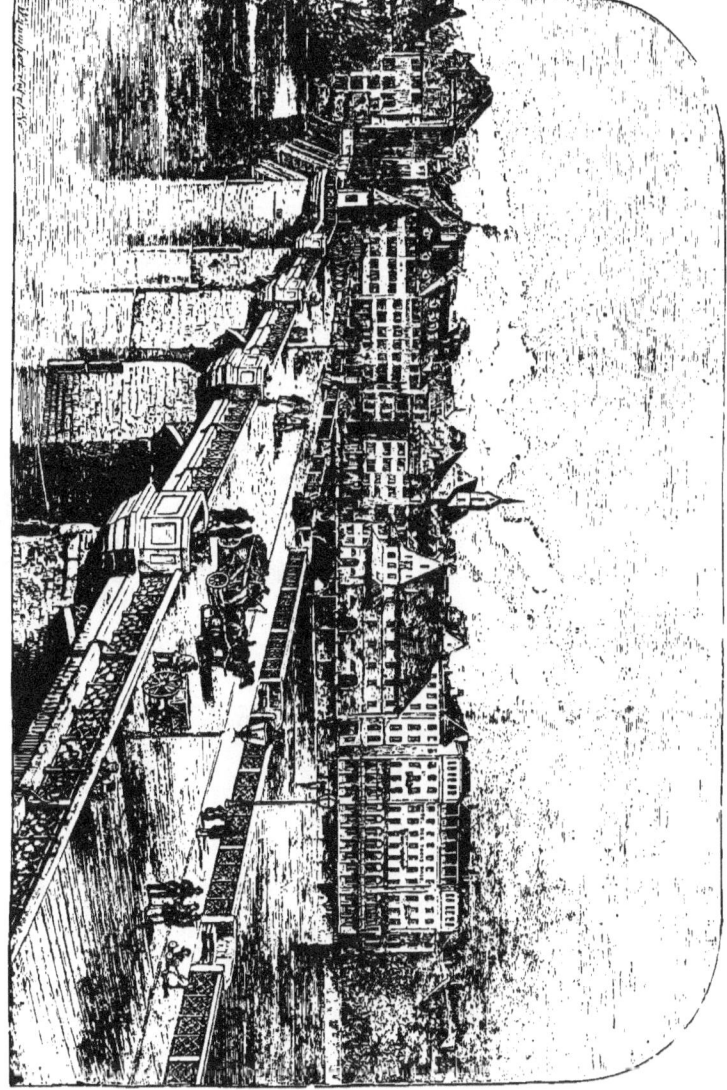

BASLE.

HIGH STREET, BERNE.

artists who cross sea and land to study the works of the great masters, or as the infidels of Jerusalem look upon those who come on pilgrim feet to bow in sad Gethsemane, or weep in sadness over the sepulchre of Jesus.

IN GERMANY.

VIENNA, FROM THE UPPER TERRACE, BELVEDERE PALACE.

THE boys reported progress on the proposition made at the last meeting, and after hearing the opinions given by their parents voted to postpone their visit to Europe until after the return of Master Van Wert. Charlie's father was not willing that he should go at present; Hal's father said that he could not furnish the money, and Will's father consented with the proviso that the fathers of the other two consented. So it was two against one; and when it was put to vote the result was a unanimous rejection.

BERLIN.

I begin my account of Germany with its capital, not keeping up the order in which I visited the various places. We had been riding all night when the city appeared before us. A travelling friend was with me when we started for Berlin. In the car with us were five stolid Germans. The natives of the soil all had cigars or pipes, and my friend, believing in the motto, "When you are among Germans, do as the Germans do," got out his excruciating cigar, so that, in a little box of a car about six feet by eight, there were six smokers, and they all smoked themselves to sleep, and the cigar-smoke was then exchanged for a nasal concert, in which six wooden trumpets would not have made a more discordant sound. We reached Berlin just as the sun was rising behind the distant hilltops, and after getting breakfast went out to explore the city.

Travellers are so enthusiastic in relation to Berlin that we expected to find a very beautiful city, and though we were not wholly disappointed, yet the place did not come up fully to our expectations. There is no way to get a good bird's-eye view of the city, and I seldom know much about a place unless I have been above it on some tower and looked down upon its streets and houses. The only tolerable view was from the Kreutzberg, or Mountain of the Cross, so called on account of a lofty Gothic cross of cast-iron erected on its summit by the late King of Prussia to commemorate the deliverance of the country from French rule. It commands a good, and, in fact, the only view, of Berlin within convenient reach of every one. But the view from this point is so distant that one does not feel repaid for the ride out to the place.

Berlin being the residence of the royal family, it of course becomes the resort of strangers. At certain seasons of the year the hotels are crowded with the representatives of government, and with foreign dignitaries, who are here on official business.

Statues abound, and that of Frederick the Great is one of muc

BERLIN: STATUE OF FREDERICK THE GREAT.

attraction for its beauty and elaborate finish. The Unter den Linden, so famous as a walk for German students, as well as for the populace, is one of the charms of the Prussian capital.

We were not sorry to leave Berlin, agreeing with a recent tourist, who says the city "is certainly the most dreary and unpoetical in Europe." The charm of Berlin lies in the society, the gaiety, and the wild and dissipated scenes, which a passing stranger does not have a view of. It certainly cannot be in the architecture or in the streets. "The sidewalks," says one, "are paved with cobble-stones, sharp edge up, if they have any, with a single line of narrow flagging through the centre, never wide enough for passing. But the worst feature is the *open gutters*, for Berlin is strangely behind the age in regard to draining. Every street is traversed by two shallow, narrow, open drains, one on each side of the carriage-way, and through these all the filth of the city flows slowly and thickly towards the sluggish river; and, as the streets lie entirely open to the sun, the exhalations arising therefrom are not likely to remind one, unless by force of contrast, of the spicy gales from Araby the blest. The city employs a set of men to wash them out daily, and keep them as clean as possible under the circumstances; but kitchen and chamber pour a steady stream into every drain, which no amount of clean water can purify. There are, in fact, but two streets in Berlin exempt from this pestilential annoyance."

DRESDEN.

Dresden is justly celebrated for its Art Galleries and its famous Green Vaults, where are gathered the antique treasures of the nation. The art collections are to the stranger the chief attraction of this great town, though there are other objects of interest. The tourist could stay here among the fine paintings for weeks, and not sufficiently admire the whole. Among the most noted pictures is Raphael's Madonna di San Sisto, which was purchased for this collection at the sum of forty thousand dollars, and Wilkie says, "The head

DRESDEN: ENTRANCE TO THE ZWINGER, AND THE STATUE OF FREDERICK AUGUSTUS.

of the Virgin is perhaps nearer the perfection of female beauty than anything else in painting." Here Rubens figures largely, and his peculiar style of execution appears in its best light. The Italian, German, Dutch, French, and Spanish styles of art are all found here, and had we had the excellent taste of our friend Mr. Oldschool we should very likely have remained much longer than we did. There are here three hundred thousand engravings, in all the varied styles of that art, and everything which can make that collection valuable.

Near by is a Historical Museum. One room is filled with specimens of painted glass, exhibiting all the changes in that art. Another is filled with implements of sport and pleasure, hunting, fishing, and the like. Another is filled with armor used in the ancient tourna ments, with coats of mail, and armor of all kinds. Then there is a gallery filled with the various instruments of war, including the arms of Augustus III., who, the historian tells us, was a man of herculean power, having "lifted a trumpeter and held him aloft (in full armor) in the palm of his hand; and twisted an iron banister of a flight of stairs into a rope, and made love to a maiden, holding a bag of gold in one hand and an iron horseshoe in the other."

In another room are fire-arms; another filled with coronation apparel and trinkets; another with a Turkish tent taken at the siege of Vienna in 1683; another with riding utensils and parade-uniform for horses; another with minerals; and so on to the end of the chapter. These galleries of paintings, and collections of statuary, armor, and antique curiosities, are very fine and extensive, and Dresden is visited annually by thousands to see these things alone.

The Green Vaults consist of a suite of rooms on the ground-floor of the old Palace, containing the richest collection of jewelry in the world, amounting to some hundreds of millions of dollars. The first vault contains articles in bronze; the second, articles in ivory; the third, a rich collection of Florentine mosaics; the fourth has large quantities of gold and silver plate, which has been accumulating for ages. Two or three other apartments are filled with gold, silver, and precious stones, wrought by the greatest skill into wonderful combinations of beauty. As an illustration of the costliness of the articles, I may mention a trinket called, by Dinglinger the artist, the "Court of the Great Mogul." It looks like a child's toy, at the first glance, but soon it is found to contain one hundred and thirty-eight figures in pure gold, very delicately apparelled. It cost eight years of labor, and fifty-eight thousand four hundred dollars. There are here rubies, sapphires, pearls, and diamonds. There are many curious things in these vaults. We saw an egg which was sent as a present to a Saxon princess long ago. It was an iron egg. Long did the receiver keep it without knowing its value or the purpose for which it was sent. One day in

DRESDEN: BRIDGE OVER THE ELBE.

handling it she touched a spring, and the egg opened and revealed a golden yolk. Time rolled on, and a spring was discovered in the yolk, and that opened and out dropped a jewelled chicken. By some concealed spring the chicken opened, and a ruby crown, all studded with jewels, fell out. This also opened, and a diamond marriage-ring was laid up within. The trifling thing must have cost thousands of dollars and years of labor and skill.

It is vain for me to attempt a description of these things. Their value is fabulous, and ages have been adding to them. No other nation on earth has such a collection as this, and the stranger walks through these vaults with the greatest admiration.

In Dresden, as in most of the continental cities, we were surprised at the children, their numbers and forwardness. Indeed babies seemed to be the chief production of some towns, and here in Dresden, we found them in crowds. Whether they are born, or grow as little Topsy did, I could not tell, but they were everywhere. They filled the streets, they were jumping out from every court; they decorated the green parks; they thronged the public squares; they gathered on the doorsteps of churches; they were lounging around the market-places. They are up to everything; ready to carry your carpet-bag, to steal your handkerchief, or beg a penny of you.

PRAGUE.

A somewhat prosy city, whose attractions are external, all on the outside. The fine Statue of Charles V. calls to itself attention, and wins admiration.

A day and part of a night I spent in the city, glad at the end of that time to get away from it, as the heavy rains and flooded streets made everything dull and uninteresting.

HAMBURG.

At home we are seldom cheated by hackmen. But our first experience here was a swindle by one of these gentry. In our country if a stranger is being cheated by one of them, and appeals to the landlord at the hotel, he gets justice, the landlord taking the part of the injured person, and setting the matter right, but throughout Europe it is generally different from this, the landlord siding with the hackman, who is endeavoring to fleece his victim.

Our first impressions of Hamburg were very favorable. It is a city of one hundred and sixty thousand inhabitants, and is a very beautiful place. It is situated at the confluence of the Elbe and the Alster.

In 1842 a dreadful fire swept through the city, raging four days in spite of all the efforts to stay it. Sixty-one streets were swept clean and clear, and with the lanes and alleys running through them, were left without an inhabitant. One thousand seven hundred and forty-nine houses were destroyed. Fire-engines were first used to arrest

PRAGUE: STATUE OF CHARLES

the flames; houses were then pulled down, but the rubbish caught fire faster than the populace could remove it. Powder was then employed, and the artillery was turned out to batter down the doomed habitations and stores. So extensive was the damage by this fire that though two hundred thousand dollars were raised by subscription for the sufferers, it did not seem to be felt in the mitigation of their sufferings, and the city of Hamburg made vast loans to repair the injury done. Banks in whose vaults were masses of bar-silver and stamped coin; churches whose walls were covered with works of art; stores filled with silks and costly goods; houses of the rich and the poor, were levelled with the ground and left a heap of smoking ruins.

This fire in many respects has been a great blessing to Hamburg, for the burnt district has again been built up with a very superior class of buildings, and thus one section of the city has a beautiful modern aspect, and an air of great elegance and taste. The Alster Basin, a fine sheet of water in the newly built part of the town, formed by the water of the Alster, is a fine square pond, with a broad, beautiful street running all around it. On this street, facing the Basin, are all the prominent and most beautiful hotels in the city. The sheet of water is about as large as Boston Common; and at all times beautiful white swans may be seen dipping their long necks in it; fine boats with gay flags are sailing over it; and at night the sweet songs of the people, as they sail about, come with bewitching melody to the shores.

There are several fine buildings in Hamburg; a small exchange; the *Rathhaus*, or government official-house; several fine churches, theatres, and hospitals.

While walking about the streets of Hamburg, I noticed large numbers of young women, well dressed, with what appeared to me to be a small coffin under the arm. On inquiry I found that these young women were servant-girls, housemaids and cooks. The thing under the arm is an oblong basket like a coffin. These girls dress very

CANAL AT HAMB

richly, with long gloves, a neat lace head-dress, and this basket covered with a very rich shawl. They have a peculiar way of carrying the basket under the arm, and there is great rivalry among them about the character of the shawl. I saw some of these girls with the basket covered with a shawl rich enough to cost more than every other article of clothing they had. In the vicinity of the markets, scores, if not hundreds, of these girls can be seen at any time during the day.

I think the Triangle would be as much interested in the market-girls of Hamburg as in the public buildings. But divested of their baskets and wares, they would doubtless appear to be a most unpoetic race of beings.

HEIDELBERG.

Heidelberg is a town of about fifteen thousand inhabitants, and famous for its university, castle, and some other things. It is a place that has met with many vicissitudes — been bombarded five times, twice burnt, and several times devoted to pillage. It has suffered from the French and the Austrians, and has a history of much interest.

The university is in the centre of the town, and has seven hundred students, who are noted for duelling and many other bad practices. They fill the streets, stare into the faces of the ladies, outrage decency, and conduct themselves in a manner that would be tolerated in no American or English town. The library of the university has one hundred and fifty thousand volumes, and it is said that in the "Thirty Years' War," when Tilly sacked and bombarded the town, he littered his war-horses on the manuscripts and papers of this library, and some others of private citizens.

The Castle of Heidelberg is a very noted place, and combines the characteristics of a fortification and a palace. It is now in ruins, a small part of it only being occupied. It has been bombarded, riven with lightning, and now lifts its ruined towers, like huge giants, on the lonely height, waiting for a final doom. There is a museum in

HAMBURG MARKET WOMAN.

HEIDELBERG.

the castle which the stranger visits, to see many antique things, relics of the past.

In one of the vaults beneath the building is a most remarkable wine-cask; the largest, I believe, in the world. It was made in 1751, and is now in a good state of preservation. It will hold eight hundred hogsheads, or two hundred and eighty-three thousand two hundred bottles. A platform is on the top, and in old times, when the cask was filled, a country-dance was held on the top of it. It lies on its side, and is thirty-six feet long and twenty-four feet high.

From the castle a fine view of the town is obtained. The river

BACHARACH (*Bacchi Ara*).

HEIDELBERG BRIDGE.

Neckar flowing calmly by, and the distant hills beyond, make the prospect a very fine one; and from the river and the streets of the town, the castle shows a bold and striking figure, as it seems to hang from the rocky precipices over the streets below.

Heidelberg has many grand old houses; and, indeed, throughout Germany these ancient residences draw attention everywhere. I would like to show you one that I saw in one of my rambles.

And, while speaking of old houses, let me tell you of the Rat-catcher's House, in Hanover, of which you have heard, and about which I remember to have read to you some time ago, during school-hours. It will answer to go with the rat story of Bingen on the Rhine, where the cruel Bishop Hatto came to a bad end.

THE RAT-CATCHER'S HOUSE, HAMELIN.

As Mr. Browning tells the story, the town was infested with rats. The mayor and the corporation offered a great reward for their extinction. A piper with his piping drew all the rats from their nests to the river Weser, where they perished in the water. The destruction of the rats caused great joy.

> "You should have heard the Hamelin people
> Ringing the bells till they rocked the steeple."

The piper demanded the fifty thousand guilders which had been promised him, but the corporation would not pay it. The piper threatened. The corporation said, —

> "You threaten us, fellow? Do your worst,
> Blow your pipe, then, till you burst."

The piper blew, and all the children of the town came flocking after him, and he drew them to Koppelberg Hill, where a chasm opened, and piper and children disappeared together. This house, on the spot where the piper lived, commemorates the rat extermination, and the fate of the children.

ADELSBERG.

This town is visited mostly on account of a wonderful cave of stalactites which is found here. Into this cave we went several times. It runs into the earth, under the mountain, and has several suites of halls and galleries. It is one of the wonders of Germany, and tourists resort to it from all countries. As you enter the cave it seems as if you passed out of this bright and beautiful world into one of death and stagnation. You leave everything that you have ever seen before, and in this cavern far below the mountain find a silent, death-like abode of icy gloom. Here are courts and corridors, palaces and castles, cathedrals and priories, ball-rooms and dining-halls, all wrought by Nature's wonderful magic. You climb into galleries of wonderful perfection, or descend into caverns of awful

WITTENBERG: MARKET-PLACE, WITH LUTHER AND MELANCHTHON STATUES.

214 KIP VAN WINKLE'S TRAVELS.

KLAGENFURT: THE DRAGON FOUNTAIN.

darkness. The lake formed by the continual drops of water is far below, and no one who has ever gazed down into it will challenge the description of a tourist of the present year. "Leaving the ball-room," he says, "we turn suddenly off to the left and move upward along a steep, narrow ledge, over the low hand-rail of which we look down into a fathomless gulf of blackness, such as Dante and Virgil gazed into from the winding path which traversed the nine circles of the Inferno. Far down in the eternal darkness we can hear the ghostly drip of unseen water, falling, falling forever, and building up inch by inch, through countless ages, new portions of this great temple of the night. All at once the dim light of our candle is eclipsed by a

IN THE CAVERN OF ADELSBERG.

brighter gleam, and a vast white mass, seemingly suspended in midair, starts suddenly out of the gloom, glittering, twinkling, sparkling like a thousand stars in one. It is a monster stalactite, at least forty feet in length by more than twenty in thickness. Its shape is that of a gigantic ear-drop, the upper part being pure white, while the countless drops of water which hang trembling from the clustering spires of the lower portion sparkle into one large rainbow as the light falls upon them, flinging far into the depth of the everlasting night a blaze of many-colored splendor. How many thousands of years has this wonderful prism been growing to perfection, drop by drop, and yet it is only one out of the infinite number which stud this strange labyrinth for miles upon miles. Indeed, it is more than probable that the most magnificent secrets of the Adelsberg Grotto are still unseen by human eye; for it was a mere chance which betrayed the hollowness of the rock at the end of the first gallery, and tempted the discoverers to break through it into the world of wonders beyond."

Not far from Adelsberg is Klagenfurt, where are a few objects of interest, and among them a unique and singular piece of work, known as the Dragon's Fountain, so called because the water pours from the open mouth of an iron dragon in a horizontal position. The whole region between Trieste and Vienna is far more interesting and more worthy of attention, than tourists who ride rapidly through suppose.

VIENNA.

This Austrian capital is a delightful city, with streets well laid out, the parks numerous and more than respectable in size and appearance; the monuments many, and elaborate in their style and execution; and the whole city elegant and fascinating. We spent some days in strolling into churches, museums of art and science, and in wandering through the streets and pleasure-grounds.

The emperor has a magnificent palace at Vienna, though he stays here but little of the time. He is comparatively a young man — about fifty years of age; and the empress is about forty-seven years old.

They do not stand so high in the affections of the Austrian people as some other monarchs have done, but no one dares speak out the honest sentiments of his heart.

My opinion of the Austrians improved on acquaintance very much. I had supposed them a rough, uncivil people; but, wherever we went, we found them the reverse of that, and I am inclined to the idea that, for general good feeling and true politeness, the Austrians are not behind the English or French. Indeed, if in England we stopped a man, and asked a civil question, we did not always get a civil answer. Often we would ask the way to a certain place, and more than once the man has passed on, after hearing the question, without deigning a reply; or, turning off, abruptly answered, "Don't know; ask a policeman." But in Austria and Germany it was not so. If we laid hold of a man in the street, and asked him the direction to any place, and he could not make out what we said, he would stop, think, try to comprehend our bad German or worse French, and really delay himself a long time to befriend us; or, perhaps, leading us along to some shop where the keeper could speak English, set us right in that way. On one occasion we wished to find a certain banker. We were misdirected, and fell into a rival banking-house at some distance from the place where we wished to go. The head of the house, a banker of vast wealth, kindly took his spectacles from his nose, put down his newspaper, and endeavored to make us comprehend where the banker we wished to find did his bank-work. Not being able to explain so that we could understand, he called one of his clerks, who, laying down his pen, accompanied us down one street and up another, a mile or less distant, to the place of our destination. The idea of a rich banker doing this civil and courteous thing in England or America is an absurdity. If we should ask one of our bankers, we should have a short, pie-crust answer, a gesture of impatience, and a wave of the hand, and that is all you would find out from him. What should we think of the president of a New

York Bank sending one of his clerks to assist a stranger in finding a rival institution? The difference is not always in favor of our own country on the point of courtesy. A Yankee would have knocked us down in some cases; or, if he had not dared to try that on our travelling friends, would have given us an impudent reply; while the Austrian and German patiently endeavored to assist us out of our dilemma, and set us on the right track.

FRANKFORT.

We stop here a little while preparatory to a voyage down the Rhine, and look at the homes of some of the world's distinguished men. Here is the house once occupied for a time by Luther, and the house of the world-famed Goethe, which is visited by all American tourists. The monument to the memory of Guttenberg is a fine thing. Guttenberg, Faust and Schaeffer stand together upon its top. The monuments of Goethe and Schiller, the statue of Ariadne, and other works of art make Frankfort an attractive place, which we leave with regret, to take passage on that famous river, the Rhine.

FRANKFURT: LUTHER'S HOUSE.

FRANKFURT: JEWS' QUARTER.

IN BELGIUM AND HOLLAND.

WINDMILLS, FOR DRAWING OFF WATER.

MASTER VAN WERT had now been more than a year in Europe, and having spent the winter in Paris, he now starts again, going northward through Belgium and Holland, in order to be in the high latitudes in the summer months. This was wise, for Norway and Sweden can hardly be said to be interesting countries to visit in the winter. So this letter is dated at the gay and pleasure-loving Belgian capital.

BRUSSELS.

A word about the hotel system that we meet in this new country. It is as different from the English plan as it is from the American. It is a combination of both, with variations. In some respects it is better than our way. A room is taken, and at the table the traveller can have just what he calls for, and is obliged to pay for nothing that he does not order. He can be as independent as he pleases. He can go and come, eat or starve, as he chooses. He can have little or much. He can call for his coffee and roll, and pay for that; or, if he wishes meat or fowl, he can order it, and the price is charged accordingly. Thus one can live much more economically if he chooses to do so, than among us. He can pay seventy-five cents a day for his room, and take his meals at a shilling each, at some eating-house where he may happen to be. But unless he is shrewd he will be cheated, for there is no meanness to which the hotel-keepers in many European cities do not sink themselves. There are many little things which are charged extra unless the traveller has his eyes open. For instance, he will find in his room two candles. The servant will light them both, and perhaps they will burn a half-hour, and in the morning he will find himself charged with the two candles at a quarter of a dollar each. The servant takes these candles, after he is gone, shapes the ends, and makes them look like new, and then charges them over and over again to others — an English shilling each. I thought I would try to be as sharp as the landlord; so at Brussels, finding that the candle was charged in the bill, I took it, and when we went to the next place, and the servant was about to light his candle, I said, "Oh, no, sir; we don't want candles," and forthwith produced our own. Thus we kept using it; and the single candle probably saved us five dollars. Well, then, as to soap. We found at Brussels that the servant had put no soap in the room. We inquired for soap, and two cakes, which had been used before, were brought us, and when we went away, though we had used the soap but a few times, and the size of the cakes was scarcely diminished, yet forty cents extra was charged for it — twenty cents a cake. As I could not think of being cheated in that way, I took the soap and stowed it into my bag, and thus saved considerably on soap, the clerk telling me it was mine, and that nobody else would use it.

We found Brussels to be much such a city as Paris, but on a smaller scale — the same *café* system, the same out-of-door habits, the same "Chateau de Fleurs" style of things carried out. The King of the Belgians, whose palace is here, is a very worthy man, much respected by his people and by the other sovereigns of Europe. His kingdom is so small that his opinion is of little weight among the crowned heads, but as a man, and a good ruler, he is highly esteemed. His chief care is to keep out of trouble with his more warlike neighbors.

We spent our time in the city in visiting the cathedral, a venerable old building; the Hotel de Ville; an old town-house with a new and superb steeple, one of the highest and most magnificent in Europe; the parks and public buildings, which are all so much like those of other cities that they do not merit a description.

The manufacture of lace is carried on here to a great extent, and we went into several of these lace-factories. I was not before aware of the delicacy of the process of lace-making, and if our ladies could stand as we did, and see the poor girls with reddened eyes and weary hands, toiling for a mere pittance to make the fabrics which contribute so much to style and finish of dress, they would hardly wish to have the article about their persons. Each piece of lace worn upon the neck costs hours of weariness and sorrow, and many an article that is deemed unworthy of a thought, has been washed with tears. The process of lace-making is very slow, and were not the poor operatives obliged to work for almost nothing, it could not be offered for the prices for which it sells. We found in the show-rooms of the establishments that it could be bought for one-third or one-half it costs in our country, the rest being chargeable to freight or duties.

Laboring people everywhere in Europe are despised, and slavery as surely exists as it once did in our own land. The operatives in mills, the waiters in hotels, the various classes of public servants, seem conscious of inferiority. In our country, the Irish girl is often mistress of the house, and the hired man not seldom rules his master. Servants are called "help," and many there are who would leave their places should they be designated as *servants*. I have read of an English gentleman, who having crossed the ocean, stopped at a hotel in one of our small Yankee towns, where the people lived in the enjoyment of the greatest degree of democratic simplicity. The story runs that he had dinner; and among those who sat at the table with him was the waiting-maid, whom he designated as "servant;" but he received an indignant correction from the landlord: "We call our servants, sir, *Helps*. They air not oppressed; they air not Russian scurfs." "All right," said the Englishman, "I shall remember that." And he did remember, for in the morning he awoke the whole house by calling out at the top of his voice, which was like the tearing of a strong rag: "Help! help!—water! water!" In an instant every person equal to the task rushed into his room with a pail of water. "I am much obliged to you, I am sure," he said; "but I don't want so *much* water, ye kno'—I only want enough to shave with." "*Shave* with!" said the landlord; "what did you mean by calling 'Help! water!' we thought the house was a-fire." "You told me to call the servants 'Help,' and I did; did you think I would cry *water* when I meant *fire*."

The chief pleasure of our stay in Brussels, centred in a visit to Waterloo, which is twelve miles from the city. We took a carriage to ride out to the place where were decided the fortunes of half the world, and where in a single game of fate Napoleon lost his empire and his liberty. All the way along, the road was lined with beggars and cripples. Almost every house we passed, some deformed creature would rush out and beg charity. Little boys in droves would run for miles alongside of the carriage, turning somersaults, standing on their heads, and performing various feats, to get the reward. The bones and rubbish of the battle were piled into a mound that now marks the spot where the battle, which decided the fate of Napoleon and

Europe, was fought. The mound is full of the relics of the fight — pieces of cannon, bullets, cap ornaments, and a hundred things that were strewn over the field on that eventful day. So little change has been made in the surroundings, that it is easy to follow the fortunes of the day, and the historic descriptions of the battle are easily verified and confirmed. To a thoughtful man a trip over the field of Waterloo is very suggestive. There turned the fate of great Empires, the destinies of great men, the fortunes of great parties, and the issues of great controversies. The spot is sacred, and whoever walks over it feels that he is walking over the scene of an encounter which changed the fate of the world.

We returned to Brussels, and having seen all we wanted to of that city, pursued our way to Antwerp, which is a short ride from the capital. Antwerp is a very interesting place, and was formerly noted for its commerce, but the city now is in a declining state. It lies on the bank of the river Scheldt, and a century ago contained two hundred thousand inhabitants, but has now dwindled down to one hundred thousand. An old historian states "that in the time of Charles V. two thousand five hundred vessels were sometimes seen at once in the river; that five hundred loaded wagons of provisions daily entered the gates; that five thousand merchants daily met on the Exchange." War and oppression have reduced the opulent city, until now it bears marks of decay in every street and square. The number of vessels seen in the river is small, and the evidences of trade are very few. At the time we were there, after our return from the interior, the royal yacht of the Queen of England was lying in the river. The Queen, the day before we reached the place, had arrived, and had gone on her way to Berlin, to visit her daughter, the Princess Royal, wife of Prince Frederick William of Prussia. The yacht is a specimen of royal luxury and extravagance, fitted in a sumptuous style, and one of the finest boats in the world. It is a steamer, and as large as the English mail-steamers of the Cunard line, and probably cost as much as any two or three of them. We asked the officer in charge what she cost, and he replied, "that is not known to the public. Such large sums have been expended on her, that it is deemed advisable to keep it from the people." Externally she is not showy. She has a black hull, with a wide gilt stripe running all round her, and looks as if she could attain great speed. The deck is underlaid with cork, so as to prevent the tread of those on deck from disturbing those below, and all the various fixtures are very fine. The Queen's state-chamber; the dressing-room of the late Prince Albert; the state-room of the Prince of Wales, the apartments for the ladies-in-waiting, and the tutors of the royal children, are all fitted in magnificent style, and with a richness seldom seen on ship-board.

AMSTERDAM.

Surely we are in a strange country now — the "land of water." Holland lies below the level of the sea, and is preserved from inundation by the means of dykes. Canals, instead of carriage-roads, serve as highways. Every city is a curiosity.

Rotterdam makes you feel as if you were in a constant dream. Delft gives you an idea of a world made of windmills. The Hague convinces you that the whole human family walk on bridges, while Amsterdam combines windmills, bridges, canals and boats, until you don't know whether you are in a boat, on land, or in a dream. There have often been fears that the wild waters in some fierce storm would overflow their narrow banks and flood the land. There have been many times when destruction threatened the country. "The winter of 1824-5 was one of the most calamitous to the country" (says one writer), "known for many years. The first of February, 1825, was a day of great anxiety; had the sea continued to rise a quarter of an hour longer, the dykes must have been overflowed, and perhaps given way, and Amsterdam would have suffered a most disastrous nundation. Fortunately, at a moment when the danger was most urgent, the rising tide stopped, and the great pressure on the sea-walls and dykes was immediately diminished, but the lower part of the town had been laid beneath the water." Nor is all the danger from without. There are constant fears that the ice of the Rhine and the Meuse may become obstructed, and thus allow the waters to be piled up for a while, and then breaking away, flow down through the Dutch river, into all the canals, jeopardizing all the tenantry.

ROTTERDAM. THE OLD HARBOR.

The canals vary in width from six feet to sixty, and are found everywhere. Towns communicate with each other by means of them. The people often dig a canal instead of building a fence. It is not uncommon, in travelling through the country, to see a man's head just above the surface of the field which adjoins the road, moving along at a brisk rate. Cross over, and you will find a canal covered up with grass, and almost hidden, along which boats are passing continually. These canals are formed through the marshes by digging out the peat and forming connections with other canals.

It is curious, in going through Holland, to see the immense number of windmills that appear in all directions. Wind is made to do the work of water and steam, being used for all the processes of millwork, grinding, sowing, ploughing, etc. There are thousands of these windmills, and they cost an immense sum of money, and do an

INTERIOR OF A HOUSE.

immense work. As you approach a town or city, you will see the huge arms of the mill, and the flapping sail, as if guarding the place from invasion and surprise. Everything is so odd that you feel as if you had got into another world, where the people lived on different principles.

To a stranger, no place in Holland is more interesting than the

Hague. The older parts of the city have the finest specimens of the old Dutch architecture, while the newer sections have all the elegance of modern life and taste. It is a city of immense wealth, the seat of political influence and power, the headquarters of the government, and the abode of the Dutch aristocracy — and that word does not mean more in any country than it does in Holland.

The bazaars and stores at the Hague are very large and sumptuous. In one of these stores, I think we saw four times the amount of fancy articles I have ever seen in any store in Boston, New York, or London. The most curious fancy articles, the most elaborate and skilful workmanship, the most tasteful fabrics of all descriptions, were for sale. Connected with the store was a fine garden, into which many glass doors opened, and the customers could go out and walk there. We spent an hour in this magnificent store, which exceeded anything of the kind we saw in any other city.

Like other Dutch cities, the Hague is all cut up with canals, and these look, to a stranger, exceedingly unhealthy. They were covered, when we were there, with green leaves and a greenish slime, and seemed almost entirely stagnant. Though the Hague is near the open sea, the city cannot be drained into it, being lower, and liable to be inundated by the waters from without.

The court of Holland is not as august and imposing as the court of St. James or the court of Berlin. The members of the royal family mingle with the people very freely, and consequently are beloved by the masses of the population. The tourist can visit the king with as little ceremony and restraint as an American can call on the President of the United States. Holland comes nearer in spirit to the republican idea than does any other kingdom on earth.

Lying between Hague and Amsterdam are the beautiful towns of Haarlem and Leyden. At the former place is a noble organ, for a long time the largest in the world; but of late several have been made, and thus the fame of this is not as great as formerly. It was

AMSTERDAM. THE AMSTEL.

built a long time ago, has five thousand pipes, three manuals, and a richness and sweetness of tone surpassing any other. The organ at Birmingham town-hall, one in Strasbourg, and some one or two more are larger, but none have been so admired for sweetness, richness, and harmonious blending of sound as this.

Leyden is a town of forty thousand inhabitants; has a noted university, a museum of natural history, several fine churches, and a really striking history. The very name is dear to us, on account of the associations which link it with some whose names we bear and whose principles we inherit.

Our last stay in Holland was at Amsterdam. This is perhaps the best specimen of a real Dutch city. It has about two hundred thousand inhabitants, and is a wide-awake, commercial place. There is no part of it where a house can be erected without pile-driving. The canals cut it up in all directions, and these canals "divide the place into ninety-five small islands, connected by no less than two hundred and ninety bridges." The buildings are good, and look substantial; though we were told that the foundations often proved ineffective. A few years since, a large lot of corn-houses was crushed down into the earth, the weight in them being too great for the number of piles used in their erection. Even the streets are guarded by legal enactments, and heavy business is done almost entirely on the canals. The city is a bay, no better, without piles, than our Back Bay lands would be; no amount of gravel can make the upper stratum sound. The palace, a vast stone structure, built in the seventeenth century, rests on thirteen thousand six hundred and fifty-nine piles, driven seventy feet into the earth.

A large number of the inhabitants of Amsterdam are Jews; and it is very curious to ride through their quarter of the city, and see the numberless stalls for the purposes of trade. There are perhaps twenty thousand of this outcast nation, who invoked on their own heads the blood of Christ; and they are ready to buy, sell, or do anything else whereby a little money may be made.

We found the people of Holland very hospitable and kind, and the quaint way they have of doing everything, adds an interest to the stranger's visit. How any one should wish to live in such cities as Rotterdam and Amsterdam, I do not see. I should think the people would feel as we may imagine a family to feel who had built a house on a raft, half way down the harbor, and did not know but the next storm would carry away their moorings. Butler speaks of Holland as

"A country that draws fifty feet of water,
In which men live as in the *hold* of nature,
And when the sea does in upon them break,
And drowns a province, does but spring a leak."

To keep out the water costs Holland an immense amount of money, and the total of the hydraulic works between the Dollart and the Scheldt, has been estimated by competent persons to have cost an immense sum—so immense, that did I not see it stated on reliable authority I could hardly credit it.

The roads in Holland are made at very great expense. There are scarcely any stones in Holland, and the road is made of brick, covered with gravel. The brick are called *klinker*, and are manufactured for

AMSTERDAM. THE LIME MARKET.

the purpose, and a road costs about seven thousand dollars per mile, and, consequently, the tolls are high and the travelling expensive.

When Holland has been invaded by foreign powers, they have in several cases opened trenches, and let in the water upon the foe. They were willing to overflow their land, and devastate their fields, in order to destroy the enemies who had found a lodgment on their soil, a novel way surely of driving out invaders.

The Dutch are a very clean people. They are always scrubbing, and you can look in no direction, but you will see the people scrubbing their sidewalks, or windows, or the fronts of their houses. The village of Broek is said to be one of the cleanest towns in the world. It is filled up with wealthy families, and to keep the streets clean, they have made them too narrow for a hand-cart. The walks are paved with small bricks, pieces of marble, and shells. The houses are kept perfectly clean and glistening from one end of the year to the other. A town regulation forbids any one to smoke without a stopper on his pipe. When you enter a house, a servant will lay down a wet cloth to wipe your feet upon; and as you advance into the hall you will find a large collection of slippers, and you are requested to take off your boots ere you go farther. Nothing offends a Dutch woman so much as to have an unclean and untidy man about the premises, and nothing will bring a family into disrepute sooner than to have a reputation for slackness and untidiness.

On leaving Holland for Germany, we began to find trouble with our money. To a traveller it is a great annoyance to be obliged to change his money at a discount everywhere he goes. In going from Amsterdam to Hamburg, a few hundred miles, the money changes several times, and unless the utmost care is used, a considerable loss is incurred. The money of some of these petty European principalities is so poor that the beggars will not take it, and you do not find anybody who is poor enough to receive it when once you are out of the city in which it is manufactured. For instance, the currency of Hamburg, will not go a dozen miles outside of the walls, and the very change you took when you bought your ticket at the station-house, you cannot use to buy an apple or orange at the first stopping-place on the road. Intrinsically it often has no value, and a bushel of the money of Hamburg, of certain denominations, would not sell to any tinman in this land, for the value of pewter in weight.

We left Amsterdam one day at noon. The Dutch rail-cars are a considerable improvement on the English, being cushioned with leather, and more neat and tidy in appearance. Just before starting we discharged the courier who had accompanied us from Paris, finding that he was only a plague and an expense, knowing less about the

AMSTERDAM. IN THE POOR DISTRICT.

languages than we did ourselves. A ride of two or three hours took us out of Holland, where the strange sounds constantly heard, and the strange sights constantly seen, are calculated to please and amuse the stranger. The Dutch are a grand people, eminently respectable, industrious and moral. No person could travel about through their queer country without a feeling of respect for the inhabitants, who have made so much of a land that lies beneath the level of the sea. The industry of the citizens is strongly marked. Habits and customs prevail which are found nowhere else on earth. The old saying which was familiar to me in my boyhood, — "This beats the Dutch," spoken when any strange thing had happened, never had any force to me until I went about among the people of Holland. They are a people, who, as the author of Hudibras says:

> "That always ply the pump, and never think
> They can be safe, but at the rate they sink;
> That live as if they had been run aground,
> And when they die, are cast away and drowned;
> That dwell in ships, like swarms of rats, and prey
> Upon the goods all nations' fleets convey.
> And when their merchants are blown up and cracked,
> Whole towns are cast away in storms and wrecked;
> That feed like cormorants on other fishes,
> And serve their cousins-german up in dishes.
> A land that rides at anchor, and is moored;
> In which they do not live, but go aboard."

RIP VAN WINKLE.

DENMARK, NORWAY, AND SWEDEN.

"THE old Master is in the higher latitudes," said Charlie, as the Triangle met one evening.

"Where is the old fellow?" asked Hal.

"Don't call him 'old fellow.'"

"Why not?"

"Because it is not respectful toward a man that we love and honor so much."

"But is he not old?"

"No, only about sixty."

"Whew! I call that old."

BERGEN.

"Well, admit that it is old age, you are not to call him 'fellow.'"

"Now, why not? Is he not 'a fellow' of the Triangle, — are we not all 'fellows' together? But, never mind, where is the honorable gentleman?"

"In the higher latitudes."

"That is delightfully clear and plain."

"Well, wait until the letter is opened. I have only seen the postmark."

"We'll wait and see."

When the letter was opened it was found to cover a tour through the three little kingdoms of the North, so seldom deemed by tourists worthy of a visit.

COPENHAGEN.

I am now in the chief city of Denmark, — "the mark of the Dane," on the shores of the Baltic. You know I have visited Europe several times, but never have gone so far north as this country before. I now propose to see this land, — and pass through Norway and Sweden, into Russia. The area of Denmark is four hundred and forty-five thousand seven hundred and five square miles, and the population is a little less than three million persons. This includes the islands and colonies of the little kingdom. The religion of the country is Lutheran, though other sects are tolerated, and the Jews, Moravians, Baptists, Anglicans and Roman Catholics all have congregations. The king must be a member of the Lutheran church.

The educational privileges of the country are great. Copenhagen and Kiel have well-established universities in which nearly two thousand students are favored with advanced education. All children between the ages of seven and fourteen are obliged to attend school, and as the law on the subject is well obeyed, the Danes are generally an educated people.

The Church of Notre Dame is one of the most noticeable in Copenhagen, both for its exterior and interior. The cathedral also is a fine edifice, and an ornament to the city. The people appear happy and contented. The support of royalty seems to set lightly upon them, and they bear its taxation and financial burdens without murmuring or complaining. The kingdom is under the fostering care of England, the Prince of Wales having chosen his wife — who, on the death of Victoria, if she and the prince both live until that time, will be Queen of England — from the royal family of Denmark. The trade of the nation is considerable, and the material wealth of the people is not small.

Copenhagen has much to attract strangers, and among other things to be mentioned is the Thorvaldsen museum, named for

CHURCH OF NOTRE DAME.

the celebrated sculptor, and containing his works. The newspapers are above the average, the *Dagbladet* being the leading one. What that ugly-looking word means I will leave you at the meeting of the Triangle to find out. If you succeed well, take the name of another,— the *Flyveposten,*— and see what you can make of it.

The royal palaces are fine buildings, and would put to blush some of the royal residences of Great Britain, while the galleries of pictures and museums of art compare well with those of Germany, though, of course, much less extensive.

The Bourse is a fine building, and the merchants of the city are as proud of it as are the Londoners of the Royal Exchange. The harbor is excellent, and would afford protection for three hundred large vessels, if they wished to avail themselves of it. The regular shipping of the port is about four hundred vessels, and there are steam communications with almost every port in Europe.

Being the seat of government, the residence of the royal family and the university city, it is a centre alike of political, literary and religious influence. To those who go to Copenhagen expecting to find rudeness of manners, or an illiterate population, the surprise will be great to find the city not only beautiful, but the seat of a high degree of cultivation and refinement.

Though I have spoken of this city more particularly, other places in Denmark abound in interest; and not merely the cities, but the rural districts and country places, have a charm for the tourist. There are some specimens of architecture, among which the Chateau de Rosemborg may be especially mentioned

It was with regret that I packed my bag and took my cane to leave the country of the Danes, where I was treated with great courtesy, and where I spent several pleasant weeks.

CHRISTIANIA.

The change from Denmark to Norway is very marked. It seems hardly possible that two countries lying so close to each other should

INTERIOR OF CHURCH OF NOTRE DAME.

be so dissimilar in their customs and manners; but, located at an inn in one of the peculiar Norwegian streets, we took time to study the people and their ways. Primitive habits prevail, and there is an air of dulness everywhere. There is nothing to remind you of any country through which you have ever travelled before, and you seem to have dropped down in a region not many years distant from the Middle Ages. Though Christiania, being the seat of government, is more fashionable than many other places, and has more marks of modern taste, yet, as soon as you pass out of a few of the more fashionable streets, you find the same dull, heavy appearance, alike in places and people.

STREET IN CHRISTIANIA.

The Winter Palace of the king is a conspicuous building, standing on rising ground, at the terminus of one of the leading thoroughfares. It gives, in its external aspect, but little idea of a palace, its plainness reminding one of our academy buildings at home. The summer abode of royalty has less of this stiffness, and is picturesquely situated on the banks of the Christiania Fjord, and bears the name of Oscarshall. It is an irregular structure, whose white walls rise in an embossment of green foliage, and forms a very pleasing object for the eye to rest upon. All the forms and usages of royalty, all the requirements of court etiquette, are kept up punctiliously, in this little kingdom of one

WINTER PALACE.

CATHEDRAL OF ROSKILDE, COPENHAGEN.

hundred and twenty-four thousand square miles and one million five hundred thousand inhabitants, as in St. Petersburg or Brussels.

The social and domestic customs of the people are all very plain and simple. The living are married and the dead are buried without ostentation, and the whole people live with the utmost frugality. If you should see a marriage procession on its way to the little church, the groom and bride drawn in a cart by a mule or donkey, preceded by a man vigorously playing upon a violin or some other instrument of music, while friends and relatives followed in a rejoicing procession behind, you would hardly know what to make of it; and yet there is something honestly beautiful about it. As in Denmark, so in Norway — almost all the people can read and write. There is as much liberty of thought and action among the people as in Great Britain. The king, who must be of the Lutheran religion, is crowned as King of Norway at Drontheim, and must reside four months of the year in this country. Since the possession of Norway was consigned to Sweden, the offices of state have been committed to a council of eight citizens of the country, who administer public affairs in the name of the King of Norway and Sweden.

THE VETTIFAS.

One of the natural wonders of the country — and the natural won-

THE BOURSE.

ders are not numerous — are the Vettifas, in a wild Norwegian pass, which every tourist in this country should visit. The waterfall has a descent of one thousand feet, and, clear as crystal, pours itself down in an unbroken stream. It does not compare with some of the cascades of the Alps in the quantity of water which falls, but there are no features of the kind in Europe which surpass this for beauty, the fall being undisturbed by rock or bank, or anything else to break its force.

THE NORWEGIAN WEDDING.

Bergen was once a royal town, but Christiania has taken away its glories, and left it to its little trade, mainly in fish; and, instead of showing the stranger a palace or a court, the people take him to the fish-market, which is a rival of Billingsgate in London, in more respects than one. The Norwegian women cannot talk so fast as their London sisters, but they can say as bad words when they get at it. We left Norway with a feeling of surprise that so few people come to visit it.

CHATEAU OF ROSEMBORG.

Again the scene changes. We exchange the society of the comfortable Danes and the stoical Norwegians for the company of the Swedes. We are in a country nine hundred and seventy miles long, and having an average breadth of two hundred miles. It has an area of about one hundred and seventy-one thousand square miles, and

THE CAMP IN THE FOREST.

nearly four million inhabitants. I have been pretty well through its diversified scenery, travelled through its forests and over its mountains, mingled with its inhabitants. Stockholm is a fine city, and all its inhabitants seem to be in a thriving condition. It is the capital, and on that account holds a superior rank among the cities of the country. It was originally built upon several islands which have been connected by bridges. The palace of the king is a very striking structure, and outstrips altogether the Danish and Norwegian abodes of royalty. It is the Venice of Sweden. Outside of the great cities the people are primitive in their habits. The styles of living, the means of transportation and locomotion, the marriage and funeral customs, the household observances, and the religious ceremonies all show how old usages retain their power, and how hard it is to introduce new improvements into old and time-worn countries. General intelligence seems to characterize the people, though the standard of general intelligence may not be here what it is in Paris or London. You boys will read in history that this fair city was twice defended from insurgents or foreign invaders, by women, long before the day of modern woman's rights. Christiana, Queen of Denmark in 1501, wife of King John, held the fortress here for five months, until her garrison of one thousand men was reduced by starvation and the sword, to eighty persons. Though

TRANSPORTATION.

at length compelled to yield, she gave intrepid evidence of the power of woman's will and female heroism. Christina Gyllenstierna held the city against the Danes for four months, and showed a heroism so worthy of renown, that when Christian II. at length reduced the town to submission, he was obliged to pledge royal protection to the people, which pledge he basely violated, and the city was given up to pillage and the people to slaughter. It was the most bloody day Stockholm ever knew.

Sweden, Norway and Denmark are so insignificant in extent, so inconsequential in trade, and so barren of resources, that they fortu-

SWEDISH LOVERS.

nately do not excite the cupidity and envy of the stronger powers. They do not lie in the track of war, and are consequently saved from devastation. The King of Denmark has strengthened himself by alliances with the most powerful nations of Europe. Maria Dagmar is the wife of Alexander III., and her younger sister Alexandra, is the wife of Albert, Prince of Wales. One sits on the throne of Russia, and the other is heir to the throne of England.

The scenery of Sweden is wonderful. Nature has been prolific of her benefits, and the tourist, if he has the soul of the poet, or the eye of the artist, can spend much time amid the variety of scenery that is found here. At one season the days are very short, there hardly being any day, and at another season the days are very long, there being scarcely any night. In winter the people are in danger of sleeping too much, and in summer too little.

RIP VAN WINKLE.

IN RUSSIA.

SLEIGHING.

THE letter of the Master from Russia came at a time when the eyes of the whole world were turned toward that empire, in consequence of the assassination of Alexander II. in the streets of St. Petersburg, on Sunday, March 13, 1881.

The Triangle met two weeks after, and found the letter with the St. Petersburg stamp upon it.

"We are to hear to-night from the scene of the recent tragedy," said the president, "shall we spend the half-hour previous to opening the lecture in discussing the event which it is likely to communicate, the murder of the Czar?"

"I move we do," said Will.

"Are there any remarks upon the motion?"

"We do not know yet what the letter contains," remarked Hal.

"It is presumed, that as the letter bears date more recent than the assassination, that that sad event will be a prominent subject before us to-night. Shall I put the question?"

"The question!"—"The question!" called two voices.

The question was put and carried unanimously.

The opinion of Will was then called for and given.

"The assassination of the emperor is only a natural event, a thing to be expected," he said. "Years of wrong and hardship have made the people of Russia mad against their tyrants. The Nihilists have engaged to destroy the throne, and break down the government, and though they may be wrong, they have great provocation, and the event which has transpired was one which might reasonably have been expected."

"I do not so look at it," said Hal. "The Czar of Russia, while an autocrat, from the structure of the government of which he was the head, was a humane and merciful man. Few men have ever sat upon any throne, that did more for their people than Alexander II. He emancipated the serfs, an act that was not forced upon him by war, as the emancipation act was forced upon President Lincoln by civil war, but it was the act of his own heart, the dictate of his own judgment. He also gave to his people the right of trial by jury, a right which, however liable to abuse, is regarded as one of the distinguishing privileges of a free nation. He also conferred upon his people many other great blessings which had been denied them by former sovereigns. I therefore think that the deed was one that nobody should have expected, and one of the most unnatural that could have been committed."

"If I may be allowed to speak without vacating the chair," said the president, "may I not suggest that the assassination was at the same time a most natural and a most unnatural event. It was unnatural, because the late czar was a humane man, and had done many worthy acts; and was natural, because he was the head of a corrupt and oppressive government. He stood before the people as the embodiment of authority and power, of oppression and tyranny. There was no legislature to stand between him and the people; no cabinet to share with him the odium of unpopular ideas, and a maddened populace looked only to him for redress, and when it did not come, it was natural that they should select him as the object of their vengeance. He was the law for eighty millions of people, and it was no matter of surprise that discontent should aim at him.

"But the time has come to open the letter. Therefore, silence all, and listen to Rip Van Winkle."

St. Petersburg.

The last thing should be first, I have been now many weeks in Russia, but I must tell you at once of the last event which has occurred in this empire. It is nothing less than the assassination of the czar, Alexander II. The assassination of monarchs is not a strange thing. The fate of Charles I. of England, beheaded at Whitehall, and the doom of Louis of France, who was executed in Paris, are only instances of a public retribution and violence that have shaded the world. Even the virtuous and good President Lincoln, of our own country, was shot while sitting in his box at the theatre. And this wilful murder of the Emperor of Russia is a like instance of human ferocity. Five previous attempts had been made upon the life of Alexander, — the first in 1866; then again in 1867. The third and fourth attempts were made in 1879, and

SIBERIAN TRAVELLING.

then again in 1880. In 1881 the attempt was successful. The emperor was returning from a review of the royal troops, March 13th, when a man who had been watching for the royal cortège, threw an explosive shell, which shattered the carriage in which the monarch rode, killing and wounding some of the royal retinue, but leaving the emperor unharmed. Alexander calmly left his carriage, and was superintending the care of his wounded guards when another shell was thrown, by which the czar was terribly mutilated. He lived only an hour, when the soul of a great man went into eternity. His son, Alexander III., was at once inaugurated, and the empire passed into younger hands, while the miserable assassins were hurried away to prison. The czar was in the sixty-third year of his age, having reigned twenty-six years.

As soon as was practicable after the exciting events of the week that opened with the massacre of the imperial head of the government, I began to look about the city, which is now clothed in its winter dress. St. Petersburg, as its name implies, was named for Peter the Great, by whom it was founded in 1703. Moscow was formerly the capital, but the mind of Peter was directed toward this place as the residence of the royal family and the seat of government. He first erected a fortress, and surrounded it with buildings for public use, and in 1712 declared it to be his capital. But it was for a long time a mean place, the climate, the soil, and the whole location being bad; but these disadvantages have been triumphed over, and St. Petersburg is now an elegant city of more than half a million people. The streets are wide and spacious, while many of the buildings are elegant.

The Winter Palace, to which Alexander II. was taken after the tragedy which ended his life, is perhaps the most extensive palace in the world. When the royal family is at home, this palace has six thousand occupants. It is as elegant as it is spacious. Its halls, chapels, corridors, are finished in the most elaborate manner, and the

SIBERIAN WEDDING.

whole is worthy of the line of monarchs that make it their winter home. There are several other palaces, occupied by various members of the royal family, and all of them evince much taste.

The Cathedral of Our Lady of Kasan is among the most notable churches. The Church of St. Peter and St. Paul has a spire two hundred and eight feet high. In its crypts below are the remains of the imperial monarchs since Peter the Great. The Isaac Church is one of the noblest specimens of architecture on the continent. Many other churches stand in conspicuous places, located so as to be attractive and ornamental, aiding in beautifying the city. Perhaps no city has three finer streets than the three principal streets of St. Petersburg. The Neva Perspective is four miles long and one hundred and thirty feet broad. The buildings are not crowded and huddled together, but stand apart from each other on large lots — a feature seldom found in large cities.

The Imperial Library is notable. It has five hundred thousand printed volumes and twenty-five thousand manuscripts. There are several other great libraries, and museums of natural science, and academies of fine arts. The University of St. Petersburg holds a high rank among the educational institutions of the continent, with its seventy-five professors and four hundred students. I think Americans generally find St. Petersburg a very much finer city than they expected, its benevolent and humane enterprises more extensive, its people more enlightened, and its industries more remunerative and better conducted than they anticipated. The city is on the Neva, but its port is Cronstadt, which is about sixteen miles distant. Statues of Peter the Great, Alexander I., and various other characters lend additional attraction to the streets and squares.

The climate is not so severe as is sometimes supposed, the mean temperature of summer being 63° and that of winter 12°. The winter cold is steady; and what Yankee boys would delight in, the sleighing is superb.

ICE TRANSPORTATION.

The new Emperor, Alexander III., married Maria Dagmar, daughter of the King of Denmark, and sister of the Princess of Wales, wife of the heir to the British throne. Whether he will be allowed to reform the government, correct abuses, and do what his father failed to do, or whether he will fall a victim to Nihilism, remains to be seen. Time only can tell.

MOSCOW.

This city is about four hundred miles from St. Petersburg, and is quite unlike it in most particulars. While the capital has a modern appearance, Moscow seems to have grown up in ancient times. The principal building is the Kremlin, which was restored by the Emperor Nicholas. The fire of 1812 did not do as much damage to Moscow as has generally been supposed. The statements in relation to the burning have generally been put forth by the French, and in part to cover their ignominious retreat. But a small part of the place gives any evidence of having been touched by fire. At the time the city was occupied by the French, the place was surrounded by immense wood-yards, where the people came for their supplies during the long, inhospitable winter. These piles of wood, and the sheds which covered them, were set on fire by the Russians, that the French might be compelled by winter's cold to flee. The French saw this line of fire all around the city, the blaze pouring forth at different points, and supposed the whole place was in flames, when in fact the city itself was untouched. Sparks reached the Kremlin and produced destruction there, and a few other buildings were destroyed and a few streets were laid waste. But the architecture of Moscow indicates that the present buildings date far back of the entrance of Murat in 1812. The masonry, the street lines, the ancient architecture, all convey us back toward the middle ages.

At Moscow the emperors are crowned. Here Alexander II. had the crown put upon his head in 1856, and here probably Alexander

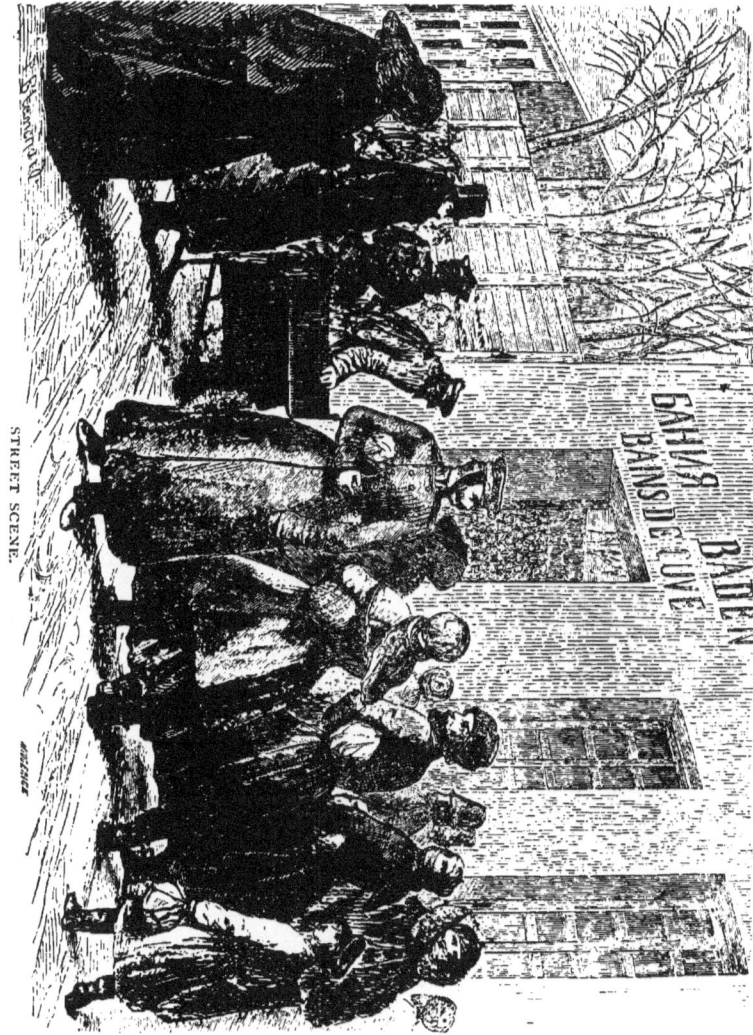

STREET SCENE.

Alexandrovitch, his son and successor, who has already assumed the empire, will have the diadem put upon his head.

You will want me to tell you about the Kremlin. That is a famous building for boys. I never saw a boy who did not care more for the Kremlin than for all the rest of Russia together. Well, this celebrated fortress, which stands on a slight elevation which slopes down to the river Moskva, was built in the fourteenth century. It is not one single building, but an immense pile of buildings, surrounded with high walls and battlements. Here is the monster bell, — king of bells, the largest in the world. Hung in the tower of St. Ivan, it weighs fifty-seven tons. Moscow is a city of bells. They can be heard ringing and rhyming, tolling and tinkling. They are of all sizes, but the one in St. Ivan is the largest. The heaviest bell in the United States is on the City Hall in New York, and that weighs only twenty-three thousand pounds, — a small affair compared with this monster of nearly sixty tons.

There are many elegant buildings in Moscow, but they are of ancient date. The palaces are grand, but do not equal those of St. Petersburg. The churches are numerous, most of them of the Greek religion. The inhabitants form a heterogeneous mass of all the classes that come under Russian rule.

A few other places in Russia, — such as Cronstadt, Warsaw, Vladimir, Kiersh, — were seen, and two of us, the other being a German who had joined me in Sweden, and who was a very clever travelling companion, found our way to the shores of the Black Sea, where we took a steamer in early spring for Constantinople. We came near as we wished to Siberia, though that region is not so desolate, nor is banishment to it so great a hardship, as some imagine. It may be that the Siberian exiles are as well off as the suspected Nihilists in St. Petersburg.

Russia is the largest Empire in the world. It has in Europe an area of 2,074,738 square miles, and a population of nearly seventy million souls. It has all the various grades of temperature, from tropic to frozen, and though there is much to admire, in the people and in the government, there is also so much to condemn that the English or American traveller is sure to feel a relief when he crosses the border into another territory.

Rip Van Winkle.

IN TURKEY.

At each meeting of the Triangle a large map of Europe was suspended from the wall, and the course of Rip Van Winkle pointed out. On the evening succeeding that on which the budget from Russia was opened, the club met, and in an informal way talked over the entertainment of the evening.

"Before we open the letter," said Will, "let us guess how our traveller gets from Russia into Turkey."

"That is what nobody can guess," replied Hal. "He skips about so that no one can tell where he is likely to turn up."

"I am not so sure about that. The Master has taken a pretty clear course."

"I think so too," chimed in Charlie. "He went through Ireland, Scotland, England, France, Switzerland, Germany, and wintered in Paris. Starting again, he went through Belgium, Denmark, Norway, Sweden to Russia, where the last news left him."

"But guess how he will get to Constantinople," said Will.

"Why," said Hal, "he will somewhere strike the river Dniester, and come down to Odessa, and there take steamer on the Black Sea to Constantinople. That will be the most direct way from the heart of the Russian Empire."

"What say you, Charlie?"

"Don't know."

"But you can form some opinion."

"Perhaps I can. Let me see the map."

"Here it is, and now for your opinion."

"I think he will have nothing to do with the river Dniester, but will strike the line of one of the railroads that I see are laid out through the southern part of Russia, and which seem to make Odessa a southern terminus. If there is steam navigation on the Dniester, it must be very mean and poor."

"Then you both agree," said Will, "that he will cross the Black Sea."

"Of course," said both boys.

"Why of course?"

"Because," said Hal, "he will have no other available way of getting from the central part of Russia into the Turkish capital. But open the letter, and let us see what Rip Van Winkle says about it."

Charlie opened the letter, but that gave no information as to the way the traveller went from Russia to Constantinople. He merely announced his arrival in that place, in the fewest words possible. But Charlie was probably right. The Master doubtless found his way down through the Empire to some Black Sea port—probably Odessa, and thence by steamer to the city of Constantine.

CONSTANTINOPLE.

This is a city of delightful romance. It is an *urbs septicollis*, situated like Rome on seven hills, that rise from the shore one above another, forming a most magnificent amphitheatre. It has a population of nearly a million souls, and the city proper has a circumference of a dozen miles. Lying at the south-western entrance of the Bosphorus, with a harbor capable of containing fifteen hundred ships, it is fitted so far to be the commercial capital of the world. Its picturesque situation, its costly mosques, its brilliant bazaars, its labyrinth of streets, its legends and traditions, its fountains and baths, all form a combination of attractions that make a visit to that city quite enchanting. There is a charm in the very name — *Constantinople*. At its mention a cloud of dim fancies rise before the mind, and dreams of poetry and splendor take possession of the imagination. Luxury, voluptuous ease, dreaming, drama, romance, are all in the word itself.

How shall I describe Constantinople, as it appeared to me as we entered the magnificent harbor? On one side, in the dim distance, rose Mount Olympus, the throne of the gods, the seat of the ancient mythology, while on the other side were the swelling domes, the tapering minarets, the glistening mosques, and the matchless externals of the Turkish capital. It is a marvellous scene, on which one could gaze for a long time without becoming weary of it. Perhaps there is no city on the face of the broad earth which has so beautiful an appearance to the traveller as he approaches. On the seven hills, rising one behind the other, the city is built, and from the Sea of Marmora it presents the spectacle of a crowd of golden temples, palaces, towers, and houses set in green foliage, and arranged with exquisite taste — a wilderness of glories, which the stranger feels impatient to explore. The Golden Horn is a horn-shaped arm of the sea that extends into the city, dividing it, with Pera on one side and Stamboul on the other. The Horn is full of shipping from every land. Vessels topped with flags of all nations are anchored there. Bridges of boats span it; gay caiques, a boat peculiar to Constantinople, are darting like arrows across it, and the whole presents a charming scene, unequalled by any of its kind in the world.

We had no sooner come to anchor than a score of porters from the hotels were on board with their cards, and selecting a name that we liked, we put ourselves under the charge of the conductor, and were soon at the landing, where we were met by the custom-house officials. They were a dirty set of Turks, who pulled to pieces all our bundles, examined every bit of paper, and unrolled every package of stones, or leaves, or relics of any kind that we happened to have. In one valise was a pocket-inkstand, and the ignorant fellow could not open it. He screwed and turned, but the cover would not come off, but he would not give up until the thing was open and he could see what was inside. This is the first case I ever knew of custom-house officers being afraid that contraband goods were done up in an inkstand. But at length we escaped. Our baggage was put upon the *hamals*, and we went rushing up into the city on the Pera side. The *hamal* is a porter who carries burdens on his back. A kind of saddle is strapped on the shoulders, and enormous is the load carried. One *hamal* carried nine valises, each of which was a lug for a man. We were soon in comfortable quarters at a hotel, kept by a lady, which we reached by climbing high hills, and traversing faded, gloomy streets.

What there is to see in Constantinople we shall now discover. On entering the streets, the odd costumes and the curious sights at once attract you. You must go on foot, for there are no carriages fit to ride in, and if there were the narrow streets would make them almost useless, especially in Pera. In the absence of heavy drays, you will meet a dozen men with long poles, upon which is hung a hogshead of molasses or sugar, transporting it through the streets in that manner, instead of on trucks. These *hamals*, or public carriers, become so accustomed to bearing heavy burdens, that some of them will carry eight hundred or nine hundred pounds. Threading our way through the narrow streets, we crossed the bridge of boats, and went to one of the high towers (Seraskier) erected by the government, to serve as watch-stations in case of fire. Every street and lane in the city is discernible, and on the top a man is walking round every minute of the day and night, casting his eyes over the city. At the least sign of fire he sets his telegraphic apparatus in operation, and gives the alarm. We climbed up a dark, winding staircase of two hundred and sixty-one ten-inch steps, and reached the top, where a magnificent view of the city appeared. Before the eye at a single glance was the famous Seraglio, the mosque of St. Sophia and that of Sultan Achmed, the Bosphorus with its ships, the Golden Horn with its bridge of boats, and in the distance the Sea of Marmora! All around were the glittering minarets and shining roofs—a panorama of great beauty.

A walk to St. Sophia is one of the first things done by the visitor. Guided by the four tall minarets, we found the famous edifice. It was erected by Constantine, and dedicated to St. Sophia. When it came into the hands of the Mohammedans, they erased all the evidences of Christian worship, leaving only the figure of the saint in the niche over what once was the grand altar. The mosque is the largest in the world, being very nearly equal in extent to St. Peter's in Rome.

You will remember that I made a short visit to Europe some years ago. At that time the Seraglio of the late Sultan was in existence. It was burned afterward. At the time I visited it, I wrote in my diary a description, which I will give you:

"The Seraglio is an interesting place to those who can gain admittance. A government firman must be secured, and a government official accompany you. The Seraglio is the old palace of the Sultan, and once contained his harem. The grounds are three miles in circumference, and occupy the old city of Byzantium. We entered by the main gate, noting the niches in which the heads of the political prisoners used to be exposed after their execution. At the main passage we were obliged to take off our boots and plod along in stockings. The royal bed-chamber, with the princely couch nine feet long, and thirteen feet wide, capacious enough for a dozen persons; the library; a dining apartment, which did not pay for looking through; the luxurious baths, fitted up with the greatest elegance; the hall in which the wives of the sultan are accustomed to amuse themselves and him; the bed-chambers; the elegant pavilions of the sultan's favorite wives; the ante-rooms and secret passages were all open to our inspection. On the outside were fine groves, sparkling fountains, and delightful arbors. There was an air of indolent repose about the whole, but no symmetry, or neat taste. We were permitted to inspect everything very freely, because the sultan having built a new palace, the wives, one hundred and fifty in number, were removed. The collection of buildings are faded, but must have been quite gorgeous in their day."

Among the objects of interest in the city is the ancient Hippodrome, a large quadrangular enclosure, in which stands the granite obelisk of Theodosius, and the spiral pillar, said to have been brought from Delphi, where it anciently formed a part of the tripod. The fountain of the thousand pillars is near by.

A day in Constantinople will be given to the Bazaars. The general appearance of these places of trade has been described so often that I need not repeat the description. Those at Constantinople differ from those in other Eastern cities only in their extent, rarity and richness. The goods displayed here are very much finer than in the other cities. There are cashmere shawls and camel's-hair shawls of almost fabulous expense. The silks are also very showy and varied in colors and texture. We made some purchases in this line, and our lady friends would have been amused to see us at it. We went into a low, dark shop, in a gloomy street. When we arrived, three ladies were there, and they filled the store, and we waited until they came out. Then we went in and were seated. A cup of coffee — villanous stuff—was brought us, which we swallowed. Then came the pipe, which one or two of our party took and puffed. By this time a crowd of men and boys had gathered round and were looking on. When the proprietor of the bazaar thought the pipe and coffee had begun to work, he brought out his silks. But we were met with two difficulties to begin with. Two questions came up which we found it hard to settle. How many yards of silk will it take for a lady's dress? As far as I knew, it might have been five or fifty-five. So we compromised on that subject, made a calculation as to the circumference of the article, and finally concluded that if there was no expansion before we reached home, the pieces shown us would be quite enough. And well they might. There were yards enough in each piece to wrap up a dozen ladies, of any reasonable proportions, and we felt safe on that score. Then the price? I know how to buy hats, boots, vests, coats, pants—anything that belongs to the male creature. Silks were out of my line, but some of our party who are very kind-hearted men, and do their wives' shopping for them, knew how much the fabric ought to be, and I wisely kept still, heard them talk, and found out how much to offer. So we came away, each with a piece of silk under his arm, and were followed by a troop of traders who had something to sell. A day spent in the bazaars is a very interesting one, and a stranger in Constantinople will never tire looking at the curious fancy articles that are found in every direction.

A trip down the Sea of Marmora, and up the Bosphorus into the Black Sea is generally taken by travellers, who never fail to enjoy it. No one will omit to sweep up and down the Golden Horn in one of the little light caiques, a fancy boat peculiar to Constantinople. This boat is a long, low thing, resembling our race-boats. A number of them skimming through the Golden Horn, one after another, gives you the idea of a regatta on our own waters. There are no seats

The passenger puts himself in the centre on a rich cushion, and stretches out his legs, while the boatman propels him through the waters with lightning speed. Sometimes one man rows, and often more. The caiques vary in beauty and richness, from the humble boat of the poor man to the sultan's decorated vessel.

RIP VAN WINKLE.

IN GREECE.

TEMPLE OF SUNIUM.

CHARLIE was returning to his home one evening, just at dusk when he met Dr. Oldschool, who stopped him, and made inquiry abou' the meeting of the Triangle which was to be held that evening.

"I wished to ask if you would allow some of us old people to come in this evening?"

"Yes, sir, of course ; you are always invited."

"But we wish to come in a little stronger force to-night."

"I see no objection to it."

"Then I will take the liberty of inviting fifteen or twenty to come with me."

"The more the merrier," was the answer.

Promptly at the hour, Dr. Oldschool came with forty or fifty gentlemen and ladies. They brought with them loaves of cake, boxes of strawberries, cans of ice-cream, and before the bewildered boys could say anything, a table was spread, the good things were handed about, and a grand good time was being had by all present. The ice-cream melted mysteriously away, the strawberries disappeared, and the good things generally were devoured. After a half-hour had been taken up in this way, Dr. Oldschool introduced Mr. Speakwell, a young lawyer who had often been in at the readings, who, he said, had a little red-hot speech in his head. Mr. Speakwell addressed the Triangle, and at the end of a few remarks, he placed in the hands of each of the three boys, a neat gold watch, as the testimonial of their older friends, and then sat down.

The boys looked at their watches, then at each other, and then at their kind friends. Whispering a moment to each other, they turned toward the group who stood enjoying their surprise, and Charlie stepped forward, and in behalf of himself and his two friends, thanked the gentlemen and ladies for their kindness, and made a neat impromptu speech, which gave much satisfaction to all the parties present. They clapped and cheered, but Charlie was not confused, but went through with his speech, after which he called the Triangle to order, to hear the letter of the evening.

ATHENS.

We left Constantinople one evening about dusk, swept out of the Golden Horn, darted through the Hellespont, and glided into the bosom of the Mediterranean. In two nights and one day we were anchored off the Grecian seaport of Piræus. Everything was now changed — from Turkish to Grecian. We noticed it in everything, — in the boats, in the styles of dress, in the buildings, and even in the faces of the people. Piræus is six miles from Athens, and it was at this place that Paul landed when he made that memorable visit to the Grecian capital, recorded in the Book of Acts.

On landing at Piræus, we took carriages and rode to the city. There is no city where all the objects of interest are so clustered together as at Athens. The wonders of that remarkable place are all close at hand. They surmount and cluster around the Acropolis, a rocky hill, one hundred and fifty feet high, and five hundred feet across, rising abruptly and almost perpendicularly. This hill was the centre of the ancient city, and is all that remains of it. At its base is the *Theseum*, a large edifice filled with the sculptured remains of Athens. It is the best-preserved building of the ancient days. Near by it is the temple of Zeus, which formerly was three hundred and fifty-four feet long, and one hundred and seventy feet wide. Beautiful columns that once surrounded it are now fallen about in disorder.

Ascending the hill, a spur of the Acropolis is found, called Mars Hill, on which is the Areopagus. It is a platform cut in the top of a rock, and is reached by a flight of sixteen steps. Here the famous court of Areopagus was held, and the seats of the judges hewn in the rock still remain. This memorable court was distinguished for its antiquity, dating back beyond the times of Solon, and its fame was not impaired as late as the age of Cicero. The judges were fifty-one in number, and were appointed for life. When they sat for judgment, it was always in the open air, that righteous Heaven might witness their decisions, and always in the night, that their minds might not be distracted by surrounding objects. These judges not only passed sentence on murder, theft, and the gross crimes, but they punished indolence, rewarded industry and virtue, and formed a moral as well as a criminal court. When Paul preached against the multiplicity of the Athenian deities, he was taken before this tribunal, and made a convert of one of the judges, Dionysius, who pleaded his cause and secured his release. Here, that grand discourse, a miracle of

PIRÆUS.

power, which has been read with so much delight in almost every known tongue, was delivered within sight of the thousand-godded temple of Minerva. This was the tribunal which condemned Socrates, the ancient philosopher; offended at the purity of his teachings, even in that heathen age. His dungeon, hewn out of the solid rock, is not far distant. It is so low that a tall man can hardly stand upright, so close and foul that one can hardly breathe. A narrow door through which the prisoner was thrust in, and a hole in the top to let down his food, are the only avenues to let the light of day into the miserable cell where one of the greatest of the ancients drank the hemlock and died.

Still ascending we reach the summit of the Acropolis. In the days of its glory it had five gates and five ascents. The principal of these gates was a wonderful one, built of Pentelican marble, and famous throughout the globe. Originally there were three buildings on the the hill — the Propylæa, the Erechtheum, and the Parthenon.

The Propylæa was the arsenal, or fort, and was very fine, and had a flight of sixty marble steps, and these stairs were seventy feet broad. It was an elegant Doric structure, more adorned than the world-renowned Parthenon. You see the broken columns and pillars of this famous structure.

Passing then to the northern side of the Acropolis, where are found the ruins of the Erechtheum, we find the remains of the temple erected to the honor of the son of Vulcan. But the Parthenon is the greatest object of interest. It is a Doric structure, two hundred and twenty-eight feet long, and one hundred and one feet in breadth. It is surrounded with columns, forty-six in number. It is built of Pentelican marble, and is most beautiful in its design and architectural finish. This edifice is yet the wonder of Athens. No person can gaze upon it without respect for the dead and perished race that reared its walls, and crowded them with the monuments of their art and genius.

THE ACROPOLIS, ATHENS.

Clustering about the base of the Acropolis are the objects of interest — the Stadium, or ancient Grecian race-course; the Theatre on the side of the hill, yet very perfect, its seats for five thousand persons remaining as of old, cut in the rock; the Lyceum, where the Grecian youth were instructed in their philosophies; the pulpit of Demosthenes, where of old he poured his eloquence forth upon the crowds; the Lantern of Demosthenes; the Tower of the Winds; the Theatre of Bacchus, and many other objects of interest. As you stand on the top of the Acropolis you can cast your eye over them all! From that hill you also have a fine view of the modern city of Athens. You look down into it from the foot of those colossal pillars, that yet stand in their ruined vastness and grandeur.

The streets of Athens are wide and clean. The houses are neat and attractive. The people are well-dressed, and there is an air of pleasantness about everything. Besides we rode through that city in carriages. We had been on horses so long, that a change, though the springs were hard, and the seats poor, was quite agreeable.

At the time I was first in Greece, King Otho I. was on the throne. He was, as you know, the son of Louis King of Bavaria. His succession came about in the following manner.

After a revolution in which the Greeks had achieved their independence, they found themselves without a royal family, and invited Otho, then only seventeen years old, to fill the throne. The proposition was approved by England, France, and Russia, and the young man was placed in power. This was in 1833. But he did not become an active monarch until his twentieth year, the government being administered by regents until that period. His wife was Frederica Amelia, of the House of Oldenburg. When Otho entered upon the active duties of his kingly office in 1835, he selected Bavarians mostly for his counsellors, which gave great offence to his people, and he became so unpopular that soon after he was driven from his throne, and compelled to run back in haste to Bavaria.

THE PARTHENON.

The people brought out his throne and burned it in the streets. The royal carriage met with the same fate, and the name of Otho became the scorn of the whole people. It is also known that the Greeks, after iinvitng Prince Alfred of England to take the throne, and receiving a

GREEK WATER-CARRIERS.

refusal, united on a Danish prince, who took the throne, and now reigns and is beloved by his subjects.

In Athens there are several newspapers well conducted, and very reputable in character, among which are the *Elpis*, *Aion*, and *Spectateur de l'Orient*.

TEMPLE OF HEROD.

The city of Athens has had a tumultuous history. It has been in the hands of friends and foes, and is now the pity of the earth. It was besieged and conquered by the Turks in 1828. On the 6th of May, the grand battle between the besieged Greeks and their invaders took place. One thousand five hundred of the Athenians were slain; three thousand men and women were marched down from the Acropolis and transported. The Turks took possession, and kept it, until by the intervention of European powers, it was restored to the Greeks in 1832. One can but feel sad in Athens — the classic city — now so fallen. The mournful words of Byron come up in memory, —

> "The isles of Greece! the isles of Greece!
> Where burning Sappho loved and sung, —
> Where grew the arts of war and peace, —
> Where Delos rose and Phœbus sprung!
> Eternal summer gilds them yet,
> But all, except their sun, is set."

Riding down to the port, we left Greece in the French steamer for Marseilles. The sea was calm and tranquil. For several days not a ripple disturbed its surface. It was like a sea of glass. We left on Friday. On Sunday morning we turned into the Straits of Messina, with Italy on the right and Sicily on the left. Towering up, far back from the shores of Sicily, was smoking Etna, while close to us, on the Italian shore, rose the ribs of the steamer, embedded in the mud, on board of which Garibaldi embarked for Venice, but which he was obliged to run ashore to escape the blockading fleet of the Austrians which pursued him. In company with him at that time was Ugo Bassa, who was flayed alive by the bloody Haynau, the Austrian butcher, whom Barclay's brewers came so near throwing into their vats when he visited England some time after. They landed, after stranding their vessel, and continued their wanderings. Anna Garibaldi, the patriot's wife, died two days after, of fatigue and exposure, while he, with a decree denouncing death to any one who should give him bread, water, or shelter, out against him,

POZZUOLI, THE ANCIENT PUTEOLI.

pursued his way North, and was at length arrested and banished. He came to New York, and remained until new revolutions called him to Italy, where he has figured since, bravely if not very wisely. Going up we passed Syracuse, at which place Paul stopped while on his way from Malta to Rome, after his shipwreck. On the other side is Reggio, the ancient Rhegium, which Paul says they "fetched a compass" to get at. He left Rhegium and sailed to Puteoli, and from there went to the Eternal City by land, meeting on the way the brethren of the Roman Church at Appia Forum and the Three Taverns. A few days brought us into the harbor of Messina, where we stayed for a short time.

RIP VAN WINKLE.

IN SICILY.

STROMBOLI.

THE first business at the next meeting was a comparison of watches.

" How is yours, Will?" asked Charlie.

Will told the time. Then Hal and Charlie showed their watches, and it was found that Charlie and Will had kept together, while Hal had gained two minutes on the others.

" Now, boys," said Hal, " I am right, and you are wrong."

" How do you prove that? " asked Will.

" Why, you have both fallen behind two minutes."

"How do you prove it?"

"Just as you prove I have gained."

"But here are two against one."

"Majorities are often wrong, and minorities right, as we have been taught by Master Van Wert."

"But this is a different case."

"I don't see it."

"How can we settle it?"

"Why, go to some standard time, and regulate our watches by that, and then at the next meeting we can tell."

It was agreed to do so. It was evident that the boys were pleased with the fine presents they had received, and well they might be. After they had spent some time in the comparison, and had expressed their delight over and over again, they put the watches away, and opened the Master's letter for the evening.

MESSINA.

We reached this port early one morning, and a number of our fellow-travellers, who had not been in Italy, left the steamer, and journeyed toward Rome, leaving us alone, to wander about for a short time on this fertile island in the Mediterranean Sea. It is separated from the mainland by the Straits of Messina, and has an area of about eleven thousand square miles. This city is a pleasant one, and the variety of gay costumes seen in the streets give the place a lively and attractive appearance. The flower-girls, the fruit-venders, the postilions, the porters, and even the beggars, seem to have a happy, cheerful look, and are showily dressed in high colors. The head-dresses are often very fanciful, and if seen in the streets of New York would create much merriment. The flower-girls look themselves like monstrous bouquets. With an enormous basket of flowers on their heads, they walk the streets, like moving bunches of roses.

This city, the capital of the province, is delightfully located, and the approach from the sea is charming. The population is not far

SICILIAN COSTUMES.

from one hundred thousand souls. As you enter the harbor, several fine forts are seen, looking as if they could send the little steamer to the bottom in a very short time. The town, rising back of the harbor, forms an amphitheatre, and presents a beautiful spectacle to the eye. Within the city, the churches, theatres, the naval arsenal, the custom-house, and several other large buildings, attract attention, and are worthy of inspection, but the traveller can "do up" the place in a very few days. In a sail-boat, we went out upon the harbor, and visited several of the vessels, of which there were many at anchor, some just arrived, and others about to sail. Oranges, lemons, raisins, and filberts, were conspicuous among the freights. Wine, brimstone, hides, and some other things, go to make up the exports, which reach, to the United States alone, nearly a million dollars per annum. Satins and damasks are manufactured in Messina to a considerable extent, and are exported in large quantities to other countries. The churches here, as well as at Palermo and other cities in Sicily, are very fine, and all have works of art in them which draw much attention. Messina has been subjected to the fortunes of war, having been taken and retaken by hostile foes. In 1860, Garibaldi took the place, drove out the soldiers of the King of Naples, and set up his flag on the walls.

PALERMO.

This is the capital of the province which bears its name — a city of about two hundred thousand inhabitants. It is walled, and stands on the sea-coast, on the north side of the island. The harbor is fine, being formed by a mole, three hundred feet long, and is a fine defence from the storms. Palermo is a city of fountains, squares, and statues. It has a much more ancient look than has Messina. The churches are fine, and some of them well worthy of being seen. The cathedral is a noble structure of the twelfth century. It is of Gothic architecture, and the roof is supported by eighty granite pillars, which separate the edifice into a large number of chapels, which are dedicated to different

saints. One of them is a very curious chapel, and is inscribed to St. Rosalia, the patron saint of the province. Who she was, what she did, and how she helps the city, I must leave you to find out. The church contains the mausoleum of Roger the Norman. Emperor Frederick II. also has a tomb here. The church of Del Gesù has extensive vaults, in which are the bones of a large number of Capuchin monks. Some of them are hundreds of years old. They stand with their monkish robes on as when they lived, and look out from their eyeless sockets upon the living throngs that venture into these receptacles of the dead.

The Palace is a fine edifice, built in part by Roger, in 1129. With its observatory, arsenal, armory, and art-galleries, it is an important structure. There is a university in Palermo, which has a large library, and was once a seat of learning of much importance. When the city was taken by General Garibaldi, he made it the head of the government, the capital of the reformed power.

REGGIO.

This is a little walled town, which figures in the Scriptures. You will remember that Paul was sent to Rome, to be tried by Cæsar. On his way he suffered shipwreck, and was cast upon the island of Melita, where various things befell him. When the spring came, the soldiers embarked with him on board the ship whose sign was—"The Twin Brothers." They stopped at Smyrna, and tarried three days, and then came to Reggio, or Rhegum, as it was called in ancient times. The place is now hardly worth a visit. It is famous for its pottery manufactures.

I visited Syracuse, though I saw nothing to keep me there three days, and after going about over the island, am now deliberating which way to go next—whether to stay through the hot months in these southern latitudes, or find my way into the ice-fields of Switzerland.

RIP VAN WINKLE.

IN PORTUGAL AND SPAIN.

GREAT MOSQUE OF CORDOVA.

Master Van Wert was sitting in the balcony of the hotel in Messina, soon after his last letter was written, when a rough, but friendly hand was laid upon his shoulder, and he was familiarly greeted by a friendly voice.

"Well done, here is Professor Van Wert! Who would have expected to meet him here?"

"And who has met him here?" asked the master, with an outstretched hand.

"Don't you know me?"

"No, I think I do not."

"But I know you, though I have not seen you before for twenty years."

"And where did you see me then?"

"At the time I graduated, in 1861."

"Ah! then you have been a pupil of mine? But I cannot recall your name, though your face has a somewhat familiar look, but I could not tell when or where I had seen it."

"Well, I am the boy who took the first prize for declamation."

"Ah! Sammy Scapegrace? I knew," continued the master, "that you had succeeded in life, become a lawyer, been elected to Congress; but with your beard and other changes, I did not recognize the slim and roguish boy in the stout man that I see before me."

"Well, where are you going?" asked Scapegrace.

"That was a question I was trying to settle."

"How long have you been from home?"

"Nearly two years. But allow me to ask which way you go?"

"I have found a trading-steamer that goes to Portugal, her destination being Lisbon."

"When does she start?"

"To-morrow."

"Do you want a fellow-traveller?"

"Certainly I do, when I can find one for whom I feel the respect that I do for you, Professor Van Wert."

"What do you do after your arrival in Lisbon?"

"I stay in Portugal awhile, then cross over into Spain, where I have some business in the larger cities which I shall visit, and after that is done, I shall embark at Barcelona for Marseilles, and I should be glad to have you with me throughout the journey. While I am attending to business, you can be attending to pleasure, sight-seeing, and curiosity-hunting."

So it was decided that the two should leave on board the steamer, which was to start the next day. The master took his passage, and at noon the next day, was steaming out of the harbor of Messina.

The Triangle, in due season, received his letter, in which, after recounting the way in which he was induced to take this circuitous route, he gives an account of the places he visited.

BARCELLOS.

LISBON.

A delightful summer voyage brought us to this port. The passage through the Straits of Gibraltar, which connect the Mediterranean Sea with the Atlantic Ocean, was indescribably pleasant to me.

We cast anchor in the harbor of the town, and spent a day or two among the natives and the British soldiers, who garrison the place. This rock has been in the hands of the British since 1704. It was ceded to the Crown by the treaty of Utrecht, in 1711. Various attempts have been made to dislodge the English, but all in vain. France and

Spain combined, tried it, but failed. It is one of the strategic points which England thinks worth keeping at large expense. The British nation pays for many such places. In the London Peace Congress of 1851, Richard Cobden, in a grave speech, alluded to this fact. "Where," asked he, "was there a nation that had ever occupied so many and such strategic positions on the surface of the globe? They

GIBRALTAR.

had fortified strong places, and garrisoned them all over the world, to such an extent, that, if a war ever should come between them and any other strong maritime power, the first step necessary to be taken would be to blow up and abandon some of them. They had Gibraltar, Malta, and Corfu, in the Mediterranean. Crossing the Isthmus of Suez, they had Aden. Then came the Mauritius, which was called the outwork of India. Returning, they had a military position at the

Cape. Crossing the Atlantic, westward, they had the powerful fortress of Halifax, ready to meet all comers. Going from the continent, they came to the Island of Bermuda, where they were laying out enormous sums in fortifications; and it was but the other day that he had heard an argument to induce Parliament to keep up the fortifications of Jamaica. He should also mention the fortifications of Quebec, which was called the Gibraltar of Canada."

Reaching Lisbon, we had ample time to look about. At once we were introduced to new customs and manners, a new language, a strange currency, and a curious people. Lisbon is a beautiful city, and with its fountains and flowers, palaces and gardens, impresses a stranger very favorably. The fruit merchants are seen everywhere, and this business is very extensive, but probably not very remunerative. The fish merchants also do quite an extensive business, and are a numerous class. The streets are not of the best kind. Many of them are narrow and filthy. Many of the houses show the dilapidating effects of the earthquake. You remember, perhaps, that in the earthquake of 1755, more than fifty thousand persons lost their lives. The palaces are attractive and strong, that of Belem commanding the first attention. The Tower of Belem is one of the noticeable structures, and looks as if it might stand a long siege, and suffer a heavy bombardment, without falling. The philanthropist will find his attention drawn to the hospitals, which are very numerous and admirably conducted. Orphans and foundlings, poor men and women, and other persons needing help, find numerous places where it can be found. The churches, like those in all Catholic countries, are filled with the pictures of saints and images of holy persons. The arsenal, the cathedral, and other buildings, are worth a visit, but hardly merit a description, after we have seen those of Italy, France, and other countries.

Visits to Oporto, Elvas, Ovar, Evora, Setubal, and some other places, took up a few weeks, and when they were over, my friend

FISH MERCHANTS.

Scapegrace, as well as myself, were ready to leave Portugal, having suffered so many inconveniences, and seen so little to repay us. It is one of the smallest kingdoms of Europe, having an area of only thirty-five thousand five hundred square miles, and a population of about four millions. The country is rich with mines of copper, lead, and iron, and only the indolence of the people and the lack of enterprise prevent these resources from being brought forward to enrich the nation. There is no reason but a want of enterprise why Portugal should not be one of the most thriving of European nations, instead of being one of the poorest and most thriftless. The soil is generally fertile, and the crops are large when work is put upon the land. But Portuguese farming is not a thing to boast of. The implements of labor are sadly behind the times. Hemp, flax, wheat, wine, and other staples, are grown to a considerable extent, but if a lot of Yankee farmers, such as have turned the prairies of the West into gardens of fertility, could take the climate and the soil of Portugal, they would soon transform the whole country. However, the exports of Portugal are not small, and, with the fruits and wines, bring a large revenue to the few who are courageous enough to work in a land where indolence is the law. There are gold mines in the country, especially in the vicinity of Setubal, but gold does not exist in quantities sufficient to excite the cupidity or the enterprise of the people. On the whole, we went to Portugal with pleasure, and left with pleasure.

One fine day we embarked at Lisbon, and, after a short but delightful passage on a steamer, reached

CADIZ.

If you will consult your maps, you will see that the place is situated on a projecting extremity of land, in the south-west part of the kingdom. It is the most prominent seaport in Spain, and the flags of all nations are seen floating from the shipping in the spacious harbor. The city has no great claims to beauty, though the Alameda is a thoroughfare of considerable elegance, and on the Calle Ancha crowds of

TOWER OF BELEM.

people may be seen, giving it a very gay appearance. There are the usual churches, convents, and religious institutions, but in these the stranger does not take much interest, as he has generally seen more elegant ones elsewhere. It is in a commercial aspect that Cadiz is famous, and I spent the time I remained here, in looking about among the vessels, and seeing the glory of the place, its magnificent bay, which is guarded and fortified so that no intruding ship could enter, except under a fierce fire. The two forts that stand as sentinels — Matagorda and Pourtales — are worth a visit, even to persons not especially interested in military matters. Cadiz is certainly not the least interesting city I have seen in this long tour.

SEVILLE.

This city is associated with the horrors of the Spanish Inquisition, which had its head here, and dreadful are the tales of history in relation to the tortures inflicted on poor, defenceless heretics. We may rejoice that those scenes have passed away forever, but every step we took in Seville reminded us of what had been done in the name of religion, in the days of that dreadful institution.

The remains of an ancient amphitheatre are found here, the seats cut in the rock, but the people have used the hewn stone for building purposes, and the structure is nearly destroyed, enough remaining, however, to tell what it was in its palmy days.

The most conspicuous object in the city is the Moorish tower known as the Giralda.

The Alhambra and the Alcazar are among the famous palaces. The Town-hall and Exchange are noted public buildings. All the public edifices are very elaborate in their design and execution, and some of them contain the finest stone-work in the world.

At Seville we saw the dancing-women so often described by travellers. I don't think the ladies of America would like to adopt such a style of dancing as we saw at Seville. It disgusted even Mr. Scapegrace. I ought, before leaving Seville, to introduce to the Tri-

RUE NEUVE DES ANGLAIS, OPORTO.

angle some of the characters we met. The Spanish Postilion is one of them. As he drives his mules through the streets, with whatever he has to draw, he makes noise enough to frighten the whole city. One would think that he owned one half the kingdom. His beasts are often fantastically caparisoned, and with jingling bells and grotesque and gaudy decorations he drives them through the streets, conscious to the last degree of his importance. The milkmen driving their goats through the streets, and stopping to milk them at the doors of their customers, present a novel sight; Scapegrace would not drink it, but I was more philosophical.

CORDOVA.

The nearer we got to the heart of Spain, the more plain became the evidences of the old Moorish times. Cordova is a very dull and lifeless place, and evidences of decay are seen all around. And yet no one can fail to see that when the Moors were here in their pride and power, their capital must have been a city of great splendor and luxury. The Cathedral, or great mosque, is a miracle of architecture. "Its founder," says Dr. Manning, "resolved to give his capital the finest mosque in the world. He is reported to have traced the plan, and to have worked himself upon the building with hod and trowel in order to set his people an example of diligence, humility and piety. The Arab historians say that it originally rested on one thousand two hundred columns. On one side were nineteen gates, of which the centre was covered with gold plates, the others of bronze, beautifully decorated. The minarets terminated in gilt-balls, surmounted by golden pomegranates. The vast edifice was lit by four thousand seven hundred lamps, fed by oil perfumed with amber, aloes, and frankincense. And enough remains to warrant us in crediting all they report. Entering at any of the doors, one is bewildered by a forest of columns which stretch away in every direction. Nearly a thousand of the original number are yet remaining. Twenty-nine naves run in one direction and nineteen in another.

THE GIRALDA.

The temples of Sicily, Greece, Rome, Carthage, and Egypt were despoiled to contribute to this masterpiece of Moorish art. The details of this great structure are as grand as the general effect is overpowering. The Court of Oranges (Patio de los Naranjas) is a beautiful spot — being a quadrangle within the walls, containing fountains, palm, orange, lemon, and citron trees, with marble and mosaic pavements — a perfect fairy-land.

But Cordova as a whole is stupid, dilapidated, and dreary, wanting what gives to some other Spanish cities their peculiar charm — gay costumes and colors in the streets and houses.

The sluggish Guadalquivir, as it rolls by the city, seems to catch the spirit of decay, and reflects the lazy, indolent habits of the people who dwell upon its beautiful banks. What a change since the days of the great Abd-ur-rahman, who ruled royally in the land now the home of the Spaniard. All the approaches to Cordova are very fine. They are along avenues overhung with fruit and flowers, beautified by the cactus and the palm, while groves of olives make shade and beauty all along the highways. To Americans, living in the cold inhospitable regions of the Northern Atlantic coast, the profusion of

THE COURT OF ORANGES.

THE SPANISH POSTILION.

tropical plants and fruits is a most charming spectacle. Nature knows no decay. The homes, palaces, and churches of Cordova are dilapidated, but nature is as warm, sunny and beautiful as we may suppose it to have been six thousand years ago.

THE MULETEER OF GRANADA.

TOLEDO.

We entered Toledo by the Puerta del Sol, the old Moorish gateway, relieved to find the place so different from stagnated Cordova. On the way in we met a mounted novelty, known as the muleteer.

Washington Irving says: "It has a most picturesque effect, also, to meet a train of muleteers in some mountain pass. First you hear the bells of the leading mules, breaking with their simple melody the stillness of the airy height; or, perhaps the voice of the muleteer, admonishing some tardy or wandering animal, or chanting at the full strength of his lungs some traditionary ballad. At length you see the mules, slowly winding along the cragged defile, sometimes descending precipitous cliffs, so as to present themselves in full relief against the sky, sometimes toiling up the deep chasms below you. As they approach you descry their gay decorations of worsted tufts, tassels, and saddle-cloths, while as they go by, the ever ready *trabuco*, slung behind the packs and saddles, gives a hint of the insecurity of the road."

The Cathedral, the ruined convent (*San Juan de los Reyes*), the Museum, the Alcazar, the Jewish synagogue, and some other buildings, are worth a visit. The streets are narrow, and nothing to boast of for elegance and beauty. What the people do and how they live, it is hard for a stranger to see without a microscope.

You boys at home will want me to say something about the "Toledo blade." This famous sword once manufactured here, and which became so celebrated throughout the continent, no longer gives fame to Toledo. The artisans who once manufactured it have lost their preëminence, and the "Toledo blade" is a thing of the past. It is a significant fact that prosperity in all these old Moorish cities has sadly declined since they were subjugated by those, who, in the old mosques, set up the altar of papacy.

MADRID.

Entering Madrid from the south, we have a fine view of the royal city of Spain. At once we seemed transported into the midst of gayety. The streets are full of people. The venders of various things make the long streets echo with their shrill cries. The bagpipe-players attract the children and women, and the whole aspect of the place is cheerful and gay.

The Royal Palace is the conspicuous object, and is well worthy of Spanish dignity. Externally it is an imposing spectacle and internally it has all the attractions of a kingly residence. It has seen many changes, and witnessed the incomings and outgoings of many royal personages.

HONEY-SELLER OF MADRID.

The *Prado* is the famous and fashionable promenade, and the élite of the city can here be seen on any favorable day, out in full numbers and strength.

The churches are elegant, especially that of the Atocha — dedicated to the patron saint of Madrid. The pleasures and amusements of the people are numerous, and as I allude to them, I have no doubt that the members of the Triangle will at once think of the sport which is most intimately connected with Spain — the bullfight. Well, let me give you a description of the bull-fight as it is described by Dr. Manning:

" Entering the Plaza de Toros, one sees a vast amphitheatre, open to the sky, with an arena in the centre. The seats, which rise tier above tier, in concentric circles, will accommodate many thousand spectators; that at Seville seats eleven thousand persons; that at Madrid, twelve thousand five hundred; that of Valencia, seventeen thousand. The seats are usually filled to their utmost capacity before the hour of commencement. A double barrier encloses the arena, so

ROYAL PALACE.

that if the bull leaps over the first, there still remains a second between himself and the spectators. At the hour announced, generally in the afternoon, a procession enters the arena, headed by mounted *alguazils*, followed by *chulos, banderilleros, picadors,* and *matadors.* The procession is drawn by one or two teams of mules, three abreast, gayly

THE BULL-FIGHT.

caparisoned. Having marched around the arena to the music of a military band, and saluted the president, who occupies a state-box opposite the principal entrance, the various performers take their places like the fielders in a game of cricket. A trumpet sounds; the president tosses the key of the *toril* to the *alguazil*, who catches it in his plumed hat, and proceeds to unlock and open the door, leaping aside the instant he has done so, to escape being knocked down and gored by the bull. In a few seconds the noble bull rushes in with head erect, and looks proudly around. The crowds of spectators greet him with excited shouts, and waving of hats and handkerchiefs. Catching sight of one of the *chulos*, he dashes at him. The *chulo* steps aside, waves his mantle over the eyes of the bull, and escapes. The bull singles out another, and another, of the gay and glittering throng, but with the same result. Sometimes he passes a man so closely, and charges upon him so repeatedly, that the fugitive has to escape by leaping over the barrier, which he does as lightly as a bird. This part of the *fiesta* is very beautiful. The brilliant dresses and agile movements of the men who skim and deport themselves over the arena like a cloud of butterflies, the gallant bearing of the bull, his sleek hide, and powerful, graceful form, make a dazzling spectacle. The slight element of danger, too, adds to the excitement. It is seldom that any of the *toreros* are hurt. But it does sometimes happen that one of them slips down and is gored by the bull in his efforts to escape.

"But to the Spaniards all this is mere child's play. If it continues too long they become impatient, and begin to clamor for more exciting sport. Two mounted *picadors* now come forward and engage the notice of the bull. The horses they ride are wretched beasts, fit only for the knacker's yard, and they are generally blinded to make them stand the charge of the bull without flinching. Each *picador* is armed with a long heavy spear, of which from one to two inches of the blade is exposed. They are protected from injury by a thick padding over their bodies, and greaves of iron and leather upon their legs. The bull forthwith charges upon one of the assailants, and is received upon his spear, or *garrocha*. Sometimes the horseman succeeds in repelling the assailant, but more often the bull, mad with excitement, is only infuriated by the wound, and presses on in spite of the spear-head in his shoulder. The *picador* must now endeavor to wheel his horse, and so escape the charge. This, however, is very difficult, and if he fails the horns of the bull are driven deep into the horse's belly. The *chulos* endeavor to draw off the attention of the assailant, and thus help their comrade to escape. The other *picador* is then attacked, and so the struggle goes on. Sometimes the horse falls dead in a moment, the horns penetrating some vital part. More often it staggers away bleeding and desperately wounded. Sometimes the horse and man together are lifted clean off the ground and flung with tremendous force to the earth. I once saw two horses staggering about the arena at the same time, their entrails hanging out upon the ground; yet the *picadors* kept their seats unmoved, whilst the crowd yelled forth its fierce delight at the spectacle. When a horse has been wounded, it is not removed from the arena. So long as it can keep on its legs the *torero* retains his place upon its back, and invites or repels the attacks of the bulls; a handful of tow may be thrust into the gaping wound to stanch the blood and protract for a few minutes its wretched life. When it sinks down to die, it is left unheeded to struggle in its death agony. The *picador* leaves the arena for a moment and returns upon another horse, which is to suffer the same fate. From four to six horses are commonly killed by each bull.

"In about ten or fifteen minutes the bull, enfeebled by loss of blood, and exhausted by his repeated charges, begins to flag. It is needful to rouse him to fresh fury. Loud shouts are heard for the *banderillas*. The trumpet again sounds, and two *banderilleros* enter. The first steps forward with a long barbed dart in each hand, gayly decorated with streamers of ribbons and flowers, and if the bull be lethargic, armed with fireworks. He stands just in front of the poor beast, and as it stoops to toss him he fixes one in each shoulder, and skips nimbly aside. The gayly decorated instruments of torture fall over by their own weight, but remain fixed in the wound. A second and a third pair are thrust into the poor wretch's neck alongside the first. The bull sometimes bounds into the air with pain and fury, sometimes roars and tears up the sand in his vain endeavors to rid himself of the torturing darts. He rushes to and fro, trying to escape or to avenge himself upon his tormentors. His hide, glossy as the finest satin when he entered the arena, is now covered with blood; his eye, which flashed like fire, is dim and bloodshot; his parched tongue hangs from his mouth. It is impossible to goad or torture him into further fighting. The *matador* or *espada* now comes forward, and watching his opportunity, plunges his sword between the vertebræ into the spine. The bull drops dead. The people thunder forth their applause. If the feat has been courageously or cleverly performed, the ladies shower down their bouquets and the men their hats and caps upon their favorite hero. The teams of mules enter and drag out the dead bodies of the bull and the horses; sand is sprinkled over the pools of blood in the arena; the trumpet again sounds, another bull enters, and the same sickening spectacle is repeated again and again with slight variations, till the stock of bulls and horses is exhausted.

"It only remains to add that at a first-class *fiesta*, like those at Madrid, Seville, or Valencia, from six to eight bulls, and from twenty to forty horses, are killed each time; that they are always on Sundays or at one of the great Church festivals; that every bull-fight costs about $2000, and that the profits go to the hospitals of the town." This is a fair description of this low and disgusting amusement, which is as common as dog-fighting or cock-fighting in America.

SARAGOSSA.

What most I wanted to see in this faded, dismantled, ruined old city was the leaning tower. I have described that at Pisa. This at Saragossa is in some respects more remarkable than that. While in the case of the Pisa tower it is a question whether the deviation is the result of insufficient foundations or the work of design, in this case there is no question. The foundations have settled, and though it has come to its bearings, the high tower presents a peculiar appearance.

It is built of brick, and overhangs its base nine feet. To a person in the tower this deviation from the exact perpendicular seems much greater than it is, and when you look down from the dizzy height, you can scarcely resist the conviction that the structure has started again

LEANING TOWER, SARAGOSSA.

and is going over, to carry you with it, but when you reach the base, you find it as firmly fixed as if it was established to the end of time.

Saragossa is on the river Ebro, and a fine bridge spans the stream, and this bridge, with the view that it gives of the tower and the churches, is one of the attractions of the place. The churches are

AQUEDUCT AT SEGOVIA.

dilapidated, the public buildings few and mean, and the city generally in a squalid condition.

BARCELONA.

Having visited Granada, where we had an outside and inside view of the Alhambra and the Generalife; Segovia, famous for the remains of a wonderful aqueduct; Escurial, where is the famous palace built by Philip II., and also several cities and towns on the Eastern coast — Cartagena, Candia, and Valencia, we reached Barcelona where we are to embark for France. This city being a place of considerable commerce, has a very lively appearance, and in the streets are visitors from all parts of Europe — several who have come from the various ships. But our purpose is to take passage from Spain on the first steamer that will accommodate us. My friend, Scapegrace, has completed his business, and I have done up my sight-seeing. On reaching Paris I shall form all my plans for the future, and perhaps at some future time shall be able to give you the results of expeditions in Asia.

RIP VAN WINKLE.

Here we are obliged to leave Master Van Wert, who found a steamer for Marseilles on which he took passage, and soon found himself at his old quarters in the gay French capital, where he met with many friends, received letters and papers from home, and where he made arrangements to start on a journey of several months in the distant East.

www.ingramcontent.com/pod-product-compliance
Lightning Source LLC
Chambersburg PA
CBHW022048230426
43672CB00008B/1105